Rocket Ron

Also by George Stone

Muscle: A Minor League Legend
Images of America: Bristol
Postcard History Series: Bristol

Ron Necciai came to Bristol in 1952 and established a record in baseball history which still stands today (Courtesy Ron Necciai/Bristol Herald Courier photo).

Rocket Ron

The Ron Necciai Story and
His Record-Setting 27 Strikeouts

George Stone

Copyright © 2008 by George Stone

ISBN 978-0-7414-4899-6

Cover photo courtesy of Ron Necciai with permission from the Bristol Herald Courier.

Back cover photo of Ron Necciai showing author George Stone a copy of the boxscore. Courtesy Boyce Cox.

Published by:

INFINITY
PUBLISHING.COM

1094 New DeHaven Street, Suite 100
West Conshohocken, PA 19428-2713
Info@buybooksontheweb.com
www.buybooksontheweb.com
Toll-free (877) BUY BOOK
Local Phone (610) 941-9999
Fax (610) 941-9959

Printed in the United States of America

Published January 2013

Dedicated in memory of Boyce E. Cox

Contents

Contents

Foreword

By Bill Mazeroski

Twenty seven strikeouts in one nine inning game. It sounds impossible. You say it over and over to yourself and it still seems so unbelievable. But Ron Necciai did it. Since 1869, when baseball was first played professionally, there's been over a million games played both in the major and minor leagues. And nobody - nobody - ever struck out 27 batters in a game before Ron did it for the Bristol Virginia Twins in the Appalachian League back in 1952 and nobody has done it in the 54 years since. A truly amazing feat.

There were records in baseball that you might have said would never be broken. I'm sure at one time no one ever thought Babe Ruth's 714 home runs would be topped, but Hank Aaron broke the Babe's mark and now Hank's record was broken by Barry Bonds. Or that anybody would ever pass Ty Cobb on the all-time hit list, of course Pete Rose broke that record. Then Cal Ripken comes along and topped Lou Gehrig's consecutive games streak, which seemed like one of those records that would never be beat. Then you got Joe DiMaggio's 56-game hit streak. Players over the years have tried to top that record but so far no one has. And, one day it might fall. But of all the records, past or present, the one I really can't see anyone ever matching or breaking is Ron's 27 strikeouts in one nine inning game.

Ron and I met briefly in spring training with Hollywood in the Pacific Coast League in 1955. Ron was on the way out of baseball then and I was in my second year playing in the Pittsburgh Pirates minor league system. Ron struck out the 27 batters in 1952 and I was still in high school back in Wheeling, West Virginia. Our family didn't have a radio and we didn't get the paper, so I had never heard of Ron Necciai until we were together for that brief time in 1955. We were all on the field one day in spring training and someone said to me, 'That's Ron Necciai. He's the guy that struck out 27 batters in one game a few years ago.' I remember thinking, 'Somebody's pulling my leg. How can you believe a pitcher struck out 27 batters in one game?' I had never heard of anyone doing that.

I remember being told by some of the guys on the Pirates team, who had played with Ron, about how hard he threw and how much potential he had before hurting his arm. It's a shame, because apparently he had all the ability to be a very good major league pitcher. Today, doctors could have operated and fixed his injury, but not back in the 1950s.

I got to know Ron many years later. After I retired from baseball, I was involved with the Pirates Alumni Association and that's where Ron and I got to be very good and dear friends. We both are from basically the same part of the country and in the winter we both live close to one another in Florida, so we play a lot of golf together. Ron's pretty good on the golf course but he doesn't hit the ball as far as he thinks he should. Ron is really a funny guy. We're kind of opposites. He talks a lot and I don't. Ron's a great kidder. We both like to work crossword puzzles and we'll get stuck on a word and Ron will get frustrated and say, 'You know Bill, they made these crossword puzzles just to show how dumb we are.' I assure you though, Ron is far from being dumb. He's one of the brightest and most intelligent individuals I have ever known.

The thing about Ron is he is himself. He never brings up the fact that he struck out 27 batters in a game. If we're out playing golf, I'm the one to say to guys we might be playing with, 'Do you know who you are playing golf with? It's Ron Necciai. He struck out 27 batters in one game.' Ron hates when I do that. He just kind of shrugs and says it was no big deal. Sometimes he downplays his record saying that the lights were bad and the batters couldn't see. Ron doesn't change. He doesn't boast or brag about the fact he's the only man in professional baseball history to ever strike out 27 batters. He is a very humble man. One time after I told somebody about Ron and we went on our way Ron turned and said, 'You know Bill, you've made a career on hitting one home run and I've made a career of pitching one ball game. Of course, you did play 17 years in the big leagues and made the Hall of Fame. I played a half a season and had to get a real job.'

People might say, 'Well, he did it in a Class D minor league game.' I tell you, I don't care where he did it. You just don't strike out 27 batters in a game. And it wasn't a fluke. Four days later he struck out 24 in a game. I mean, pitchers in that league have been throwing for years and nobody ever struck out 27 in a game. The most I ever saw in a game was when Bob Veale pitched for us against the Phillies in 1965 and struck out 16. I thought that was a lot of strikeouts, and it was.

I may be proven wrong one day but I truly believe that Ron's 27 strikeouts is a record no one will ever equal again. Ron Necciai did an amazing thing. And it couldn't have happened to a nicer guy either. I'm very lucky to call him a friend.

Bill Mazeroski

HOF 01

Prologue

Ron Necciai steers the silver BMW onto the gravel parking lot of his favorite lunchtime bistro and before stepping from the car the slender 72-year-old suggests a bowl of Italian wedding soup as an appetizer to what is intended to be a light lunch.

"Anything you get here is delicious, but the Italian wedding soup is fantastic," says Necciai, who speaks with passion using hand gestures as he walks gingerly over the loose gravel and past the Coca-Cola sign advertising the box-like building as Lenzi's Italian Restaurant.

Tuesday's specials are hand-scrawled in Sharpie black on several pieces of paper adhered with Scotch tape to the double glass doors leading into Lenzi's. Necciai swings open the door and appears oblivious to the $4.99 spaghetti and meatball special begging to gain the customer's attention. Necciai is a regular at Lenzi's and he knows exactly what to order before taking that first step over the threshold.

Lenzi's is located at 228 Gee Street, just off the main drag of Monongahela, Pennsylvania. The restaurant was once positioned a hundred feet to the south, but that was before the city erected a new bridge to span Pigeon Creek back in 1962. And the restaurant has changed little over the past four decades. Seven tables can seat up to 28 customers and that doesn't count the 10 chrome stools lining the counter separating the dining area from the kitchen. Customers from anywhere in the restaurant can see through to the kitchen where the cook seems to be preparing a dozen dishes at one time and whose hands move swiftly like those of a Vegas card dealer. And, at the same time, the chef converses with patrons at the counter, discussing subjects from politics to the movies.

Lenzi's is a family owned business. John Timko is a third generation operator and wears the title of owner, cook, maintenance man and fill-in-the-blank. One must be versatile when working as a restaurateur and John Timko is definitely versatile just as his grandfather Piacentino Lenzi must have been when he opened the restaurant in 1940 after immigrating from Montecatini Alto, Italy. Today, Timko's two sons – John Jr. and Tim – carry on the tradition helping dad run the restaurant which Timko's aunt Jean passed on to her nephew about the time Chubby Checker was swiveling to The Twist. Lenzi's is a tradition in Monongahela. It has endured hard economic times and it even survived the flood of 1985 when Pigeon Creek, which flows into the Monongahela River, overflowed its banks and nearly swept the restaurant down stream.

Lenzi's serves Italian cuisine with recipes handed down from generation to generation specializing in homemade pomodoro sauce, thick and red and hearty when poured generously over ravioli or homemade tripe, polentia, or gnocchi. Customers are also held hostage at Lenzi's because there is no leaving the premises without sampling Louise's - John Sr.'s wife - homemade Italian Ricotta cake, rice pudding or bread pudding.

Two menus are brought to the table but Necciai leaves his untouched as he orders an eggplant hoagie. "If you've never tried this, you need to," Necciai says in a manner that made me not want to disagree since he was picking up the tab.

The pace is slow at Lenzi's on a Tuesday afternoon. It's two o'clock and the lunchtime rush is over. Necciai chats with Howard Springer, the retired chief of police for Carroll Township who, like Necciai, is a frequent visitor here. Irwin Yates, a retired barber from nearby Donora, stops by the table and asks Necciai about his golf game.

"Thought maybe you were out playing golf?" Yates asks.

Necciai grimaces, "No golf for a while. My back is acting up again."

Clem Gigliotti, a construction contractor, sits two tables over near the wall.

"I haven't seen you in a while Ron, where you been?" Gigliotti asks.

"I was just here day before yesterday Clem, don't you remember?" Necciai deadpans pretending to be annoyed.

"Sure I remember, but you weren't here yesterday," Gigliotti fires back.

Louise is waiting our table and brings the eggplant hoagies along with two bowls of Italian wedding soup – a mixture of chicken broth, spinach, very small Italian meatballs and acini di pepe pasta. After tasting a few scoops of the soup, Necciai waits for a reaction from someone who had never tasted this very delectable dish before. "Well, was I right about the wedding soup?"

Necciai asks with the answer being an obvious yes, the soup was superb.

After a leisurely lunch, it was back into the BMW for a tour of Monongahela (pronounced Mon-non-ga-HELL-a and not Moe-non-ga-HAY-la nor Moe-non-ga-HE-la) which is located 30 miles south of Pittsburgh. Necciai has lived most of his life around Monongahela, the name of which is derived from the Delaware Indian words of Monona (high clayey banks) and Henna (swift waters). Necciai was actually born in Gallatin, in 1932, across the Monongahela River from the town of Monongahela and just a short distance down Bunola River Road.

The name Necciai (pronounced NETCH-EYE) takes up a couple of inches in the Monongahela phone directory and they all are related as one might expect. The Necciai journey to America began with Agostino Necciai and wife Armeda arriving in the United States in 1893 from Montecatini Alto in Tuscany, Italy traveling to New York City and from New York to settle in Fredericktown, Pa., about 30 miles south of Monongahela. Fredericktown was their destination as word had come from friends about ready and available work to be found in the coal mines of the region. They all were working for a slice of that American dream. It was in 1905, upon settling in their new homeland, that Agostino and Armeda began their own family with the birth of son Attilio.

A few miles north, in Manown, Andrew Gondoly and wife Mary had just arrived from Snina, Czechoslovakia to make their own way in the new country. Andrew first went to work in the Manown coal mines before opening his own grocery store in 1926. It was in 1910 that the Gondolys were blessed with a daughter – Anna -

and as she matured into a pretty, young lady, Anna assisted her father in the grocery store.

In the years since Attilio's birth, the Necciais had left Fredericktown and moved north to Gallatin. Attilio grew into a strong young man and found steady work in the Coshoston Iron Mill in Manown. After work and while on his way back home, Attilio would sometimes stop to make a purchase at Andrew Gondoly's grocery store. On one such visit Attilio met Anna and would thereafter find any excuse to stop by the store. Anna and Attilio fell in love and were married in 1927. Anna and Attilio moved to Gallatin and in 1928 daughter Violet was born. The Necciai family would continue to grow as Attilio Jr. was born in 1930 followed by Ronald Andrew in 1932 and Sandra in 1935.

When Ron was only five years old tragedy struck the Necciai family. The elder Attilio, just 31 years old, became bedridden with pneumonia and would die from the illness on May 4, 1937. "I barely remember because I was so young but I do remember that life wasn't easy after my father died," Necciai says sitting behind the steering wheel and still in the parking lot at Lenzi's. "As a matter of fact, life was very hard for us. We were poor, but the thing about that was we didn't know we were poor. We did OK. Our family got along and we worked. All of the kids worked."

With four children and no head of the house and with limited income, the pressure was on 27-year-old Anna to put her children up for adoption. But the strong-willed Anna never considered that being an option, as her children were the most important part of her life. While money was scarce, there was enough love to keep this family together and Anna was doing everything humanly possible to make sure there was food on the table day after day. Anna found odd jobs cleaning houses around Monongahela. She would walk the mile and a half from her home in Manown, work all day for a meager 35 to 50 cents, and then walk back home to take care of the kids after school. Necciai struggles to hold back the tears as his voice quivers in remembering how his mother – whom he calls his hero – held the family together. "People talk about welfare, well I know what welfare is because we were on it," Necciai says unashamedly. "My mother, she was my hero. She'll always be my hero...."

Ron did his part to help the family ward off the bill collectors. Down at the combustion mill, pig iron was used in casting molds and little pieces would fall off into the black dirt outside. Ron and brother Attilio (Til for short) would take a wooden keg, fill it with these little bits and pieces of pig iron and then carry the keg down to Axleton and receive 10 cents in return. Til also worked in the pro shop at the Country Club and when Ron was 12, Til was able to get his little brother a job caddying. Ron and Til would walk from Manown over to Monongahela and often would hitch a ride up Cemetary Hill to the Country Club. Ron would caddy all day. "It wasn't unusual for Til and I to bring home more money than mother," Necciai says. And, when the western Pennsylvania weather turned bitter cold and the golf club shut down for the season, Ron and sister Violet would clean Grodecor's Drug Store in Monongahela after school as well as the Top Hat nightclub in Gallatin on Saturdays.

It wasn't at all unusual for the Necciais to bring home government surplus food which was often given out to the needy at Axleton and Sunnyside.

As for medical care, a visit to the doctor had to be for something serious such as the time Ron, who was about 11 or 12, had his tonsils removed. Necciai recalls he and his mother being given coupons, which served as passes to ride the streetcar from Monongahela to Pittsburgh to have the operation at the children's hospital.

Those lean beginnings made an impact on Necciai. It's not easy reliving those days. He freely admits, however, that those struggles made him tougher. It is why Necciai has never taken what he has today for granted.

Necciai turns the ignition and steers the BMW off the gravel parking lot and hits route 88 before connecting to highway 837 heading south.

"Use to be nothing across the river but mills," Necciai says as he watches the road with one eye and the other eye trained on the passing landmarks. "That building over there was on a slate dump and there was a baseball field there. We called it Yankee Field. I played independent baseball there when I was 16 or 17. What you see here is all that's left of Monongahela. All the jobs are gone and all the young people are gone."

Without ever noticing a drastic change to denote leaving one town and entering another, it's difficult to really tell when you leave Monongahela and enter Donora – the birthplace of Stan Musial.

"Stan's a great guy. Just super. He came back here several years ago but he doesn't come back very often. There's nothing to come back to. All that white stuff over there is scrap from the steel mill. Very coarse scrap called slag. That mill over there made nails for U.S. Steel. Right up there is where the galvanizing took place. Called it the tin mill. On the other end was the zinc works. In 1948 there was a huge inversion and killed 20-25 elderly people because of the smog that came in."

We drove a couple of miles, crossed the Monongahela River and headed north on route 136 or Rainbow Run Road.

"All this country is undermined. The Black Diamond Mine used to be here. It's not unusual to find a place that's sunk in because of the ground giving way. We're passing through Gallatin now and the next little town is Manown. I was born in Gallatin but when I was about three we moved to Manown because it was closer to the mill where my father worked. We lived there until 1941 and then we moved back to Gallatin. The house I grew up in is gone now. Where we used to play ball is now a park along the river."

The drive came upon a row of frame houses constructed in the early 1900s and all very obviously designed from the same blueprints.

"Those were mill houses or company houses as they were called. People who worked in the mills lived in those houses owned by the company. As long as you lived in these houses and paid the rent you had a job. You can see what's left of these houses. They're all alike. One just like the other. They're all waiting for the mills to come back and they're not coming back. When the mills were running up to 1975, this place was booming. People couldn't find enough things to spend their money on. But that's gone now.

"Thirty thousand people worked in this entire span from Allenport down river eight miles. Look at the houses. Five in a row and what's the difference in them? Two yellow, two green and one white. They're privately owned now. This used to be a fabulous place but there's no industry here anymore. We used to go to Donora to play football, baseball and basketball. I remember seeing trains go by with 200 cars of coal. We used to steal chunks off the train when it came through Manown to heat our house in the winter and to cook with."

The drive continued, Necciai was silent for a moment and then proceeded in his role as the tour guide.

"This is Gallatin Sunnyside. I went to grade school right over there from the fourth grade to the eighth. Before that I went to Axleton grades one through three. Where those orange traffic cones are was a six-room school with eight grades. The kids would pick up coal along the tracks in back of the school and put the coal in a bucket that was beside the stove. We're leaving Sunnyside now and it becomes Manown and that house over there was where I used to live. Back behind the trees was our outhouse. We didn't have water. We had electricity but no water. We carried the water up a hill to the house. This was one of two houses I was raised in. Now right over there was a little house where that tree is that I was born in but the house isn't there anymore."

Necciai pulled off the side of the road and shifted the BMW into park but left the engine running.

"Down there, along the river we used to play soccer and baseball. I spent a lot of time there. Now it's a township park. When I lived here nobody locked their doors. Nobody worried about where their kids were. There's a lot of good memories here."

Necciai was silent for a moment gazing out the window as if lost in those memories. Without saying a word, he put the car into drive and pulled back onto the asphalt. As the car motors past a utility crew working on a broken water line spouting water onto the road, an empty building looms to the far left.

"This was Combustion where my father worked. Over there is where we used to pick the pig iron by the buckets and resell it. And right next to it used to be Liggett Spring and Axle. And right over there was the little school where we could go to get our government surplus food."

The day was getting long so Necciai drove across the Monongahela Bridge, past Lenzi's and on to Main Street easing through downtown Monongahela. Monongahela has suffered since the demise of the mills but it has adjusted to the times.

Monongahela actually came into being seven years before the nation was born when William Nowland, Peter Froman and James Linnes purchased tracts of land at the mouth of the Pigeon Creek. It was Joseph Parkinson, a trader and ferry operator, who historians say actually founded Monongahela. Before it was Monongahela, the town was called Parkinson's Ferry, Williamsport and then Monongahela City. Monongahela was made the official name on April 1, 1837.

"When I was growing up the town was made up of churches and bars," Necciai says as he stopped for a traffic light. "Half the bars are gone now and so are most of the churches. There's a lot of antique stores and lots of people come down from Pittsburgh to shop."

The drive through Monongahela is not hurried. No one honks their horn and people actually smile when you look their way.

"It's definitely small town atmosphere," Necciai says. "That's the way I like it. Monongahela ends here and this is where New Eagle starts. Coates Restaurant was right there. The chief of police owned it. We used to say that if anybody got served bad food the chief ought to let our families off easy if they were caught speeding through New Eagle.

"There was where we played high school and Legion ball. Called it Quinn Park. If you hit the ball on the road it would be a home run. That building on the right used to be the high school and on the left and right of this entrance and paved road was our high school football field. We lived in Manown and we'd walk over here to school. There were streetcars that ran from Charleroi to downtown Pittsburgh; they've been gone for over 30 years. If the streetcar wasn't full, the operator would let us on and then let us off down at 12th street so we wouldn't have to walk the 12 blocks to school. Here we are at Fourth Street where we started our drive. Now you can say you got the nickel tour of the area and got cheated out of four cents."

It was now late afternoon when Necciai pulled into the garage adjacent to his home. Martha was back at the house and greeted her husband at the door with news that the realtor wanted him to call. After living at 201 Rosewood Drive for 28 years, the Necciais were selling and moving to a condo.

"We've been awful busy the last few months trying to sell," Necciai says. "It's been hard on Martha. She actually worked with the architect in designing the house. We hate leaving but we know we're getting older. There's too many stairs here."

Martha and Ron have been married 50 years. It all started back at Monongahela High School when Martha was a freshman and Ron a senior. "I went to school with Martha's brother Bobby. We played sports together and I never even knew he had a younger sister. Martha and I began dating until I left to play ball in the minors. But one day I stopped by the school to see my old coaches and teachers and happened to run into Martha. She and a friend were outside on their lunch break. I was on my way to Forbes Field and I asked them if they'd like to ride up there with me. They did but they got detention because they were supposed to be in school."

The rest is history. The Necciais have raised three children – Susan, Mark and Kirk.

The hard times Necciai grew up in are most difficult to fully understand. Today Necciai lives comfortably, playing golf when he wants and, in retirement, he can look back on life and feel really good about his accomplishments. He loves his wife and family and community in which he's been a part of for nearly 73 years. He served on the school board for the Ringgold School District from 1969 to 1975 and is concerned about the future and direction his town is heading.

Enter the Necciai house and everything is in its place. Try to guess the head of the household's past occupation and you are given no clue. There is one room in the basement with picture albums, photos on the wall and plaques. It all tells one small segment of Necciai's life. A segment that intrigues others, but not Necciai. A picture hangs on the wall of a skinny young man wearing a baseball cap with his Adam's apple protruding and a smile as natural as the man behind the smile. The picture was taken over 50 years ago when young 19-year-old Ronald Necciai's occupation was that of a professional baseball player. It was a career which was way too short, but the teen-ager left a mark on baseball which would appear to be something out of a dime store novel.

Ask Ron Necciai and he'll tell you the story. It's the story of a little bit of baseball history that took place in a small town in Virginia. A long way from Gallatin and a long way from a dream.

Chapter 1

Pitiful Pirates

Billy Meyer sat in the Pittsburgh Pirates dugout at Forbes Field as if frozen to the pine bench, silent and motionless. With arms folded across his chest and the back of his throbbing head resting against the concrete wall, Meyer's blood shot eyes were shaded by the bill of his cap pushed low over his forehead.

Meyer, the abject manager of the Pirates, had more than his share of sleepless nights over the past month. Tonight would be no different, thanks to a five-hitter by Boston's Warren Spahn. Meyer's condition wasn't clinically defined but it didn't require a medical degree to diagnose that Meyer was suffering from a lengthy losing streak. Meyer tilted his head forward slightly and peeked from under his cap. The scoreboard, located down the left field line, remained lit as a reminder of yet another night of failure for Pittsburgh - BOSTON 5, PIRATES 1. Meyer could hear the hoarse ranting of a disgruntled fan somewhere in the stands behind the dugout shouting at no one in particular, but venting his voice for all Pirates' fans around the city: "The Pirates stink.

1

STINK!" Meyer could relate to the fan's frustration and there were times he himself felt like uttering that same sentiment.

The loss to Spahn and the Braves was the 10th straight for Meyer's club in what was evolving into an abominable beginning for the 1952 season. It was only April 29 and the Pirates were 2-12. Meyer's ulcers were burning deep in his gut. He was sweating profusely despite a cool night in Pittsburgh with the thermometer hovering in the upper 40s. "Two wins," Meyer mumbled under his breath. "Two lousy wins and twelve lousy losses and it's not even May." Ulcers thrive on such misery.

Over the course of the past four games, the Pirates had been outscored 23-5. The Pirates had no offense and the pitching was being pummeled. With the exception of three, maybe four players, Meyer would have been justified in requesting that the ownership send the remainder of the squad west to make an even swap with the Pirates' Triple-A team at Hollywood of the Pacific Coast League. As a matter of fact, Meyer probably would not have bet one cent that the current major league Pirates could win even in the PCL.

Meyer, as he remained rigid in the dugout, realized fully that there was only so much he could do with the aggregation of players he was handed. Still, it didn't seem fair that Chuck Dressen in Brooklyn could have the likes of Hodges, Robinson, Reese, Snider, Campanella, Erskine and Loes all in one clubhouse. Or Leo Durocher in New York could make out a lineup card with Mays, Irvin, Dark, Maglie and Jansen. And in St. Louis Eddie Stanky had no right to complain with names like Schoendienst, Slaughter, Musial and Sisler.

Meyer cringed that a team so miserable as the Pirates would have the audacity to sink its cleats into the hallowed ground of

Forbes Field. The very same piece of earth where the likes of Honus Wagner and the Waner brothers and Deacon Phillippe once roamed for a Pittsburgh organization which at one time was among the elite of the National League. Those days were long gone. There was no Wagner or anyone named Waner and no Phillippe around in 1952. These Pirates were making a mockery of the organization. A sacrilege no less.

Ten straight defeats. Somewhere along the line you luck up and win one. But not these Pirates. The New York Giants a year earlier had lost 11 straight games during a miserable stretch of the season but proceeded to claim the National League pennant. These Pirates were not in the same class as the Giants who the year before won the National League title over the Dodgers thanks to Bobby Thomson's dramatic home run in the playoffs. The New York Giants of 1951 were much more capable of winning 11 straight than they were of losing 11 straight. The Pirates were sitting on 10 straight losses and Meyer had no reason to believe that the streak might not hit 20 or 30 straight losses.

With eyes closed and head back, Meyer was hoping this nightmare would vanish like a bad dream in the middle of the night and that he would wake up in the morning and the Pirates would be perched on top of the NL standings. As Meyer opened his eyes with the lights of Forbes still blaring down on the ground crew manicuring the infield, the regular beat writers were beginning to gather around pouncing on him like buzzards on a dead carcass stoking Meyer's already inflammatory ulcers.

Only the day before, Meyer visited his personal physician. Meyer had one question for his doctor: What would alleviate the discomfort of those ulcers? The doctor reportedly advised Meyer the best treatment would be for the Pirates to start winning. Meyer, in turn, asked what would be the second best treatment? Unfortunately for Meyer the burning ulcers would erupt on a regular basis, aggravated by his day-to-day misery of managing a team which now, 55 years later, has the dubious distinction of being one of the worst in major league baseball history. The stress and frustration were eating away at Meyer, emotionally and physically.

Sports statistician Harry Hollingsworth, back in 2000, developed a computer ranking of major league teams and he listed the 1952 Pirates as the sixth worst team of all time based on Pittsburgh's 112 losses in 154 games. These Pirates were legitimate losers.

As Meyer was attempting to bury a disappointing 1951 season heading into spring training in preparation for the 1952 campaign, he was counting on his club improving on its 64-90 record. Seventy wins would be a realistic goal. In private, Meyer never entertained optimism that this inexperienced and underdeveloped collection of ballplayers, several of whom had not yet even started to shave, would compete with the rest of the National League.

In public, Meyer walked and talked the company line choosing his words carefully when making observations about the Pirates' prospects for the upcoming season. There was little doubt in Meyer's opinion the team would struggle to make it out of the second division and he wasn't saying anything to the contrary when asked. The won-loss column could be a virtual repeat of 1951 as the Pirates front office had made no trades to improve the club and there was no prospect dressed as Superman waiting in the wings to make the jump from the minor leagues to the majors. Much to Meyer's agony, he would eventually have more doctor visits in April than the Pirates would have wins.

No matter how bad the preseason outlook may be for a team, the public relations person seems to find some glimmer of optimism in which to puff up press releases fed to the hometown media. The idea was to make the team sound as good as possible to enhance ticket sales back home when snow still blanketed the ground. It wasn't that easy for the Pirates. The baseball prognosticators predicted a dismal season for Pittsburgh in 1952. The writers could not paint a rosy picture of the Pirates as the team bungled its way through spring training. Not even Van Gogh could paint a positive picture of these Pirates. Writers, club officials and fans were not optimistic about their team's fortunes. Maybe, just maybe, with a little luck the Pirates might finish seventh in the eight-team league, which was exactly where the Bucs finished 1951, just ahead of the Chicago Cubs with two more wins. There was no doubt it was going to be a long year in Pittsburgh. An indication of just how long the season would be came sooner than expected.

Fans avoided Forbes Field in the early weeks as if a quarantine sign had been posted on every ticket booth. Cold temperatures around the three rivers, along with a poor prognosis for the season, were deterrents to early ticket sales. Meyer and the Pirates were hearing from the frustrated fans before the final frost had settled upon the Alleghenies as the Pirates wasted very little time in spiraling into a rapid descent into the cellar of the National League.

Meyer was an affable man. He was difficult to anger and generally had a twinkle in his eye and a quip on his lips. The players loved him. The front office loved him. The fans loved him. Even the writers loved him. Meyer began a career in professional baseball in 1909 at the age of 17 and developed into a skilled receiver behind the plate, he just couldn't hit. The Chicago White Sox brought Meyer to the big leagues for a brief trial in 1913, he returned to the minors in 1914-15 but resurfaced in the major leagues in 1916-17 with Connie Mack's Philadelphia Athletics. Meyer became familiar with every splinter on the dugout bench, as he was second string to Wally Schang, who was entering the fourth season of what would become a 19-year career in the majors. Meyer made the most out of his time in the big leagues sticking like glue to Mack and absorbing every nuance of the game and studying the fundamentals of each position and the intricacies of strategy. Mack recognized a special quality in Meyer. Meyer had a unique understanding of the game and a hunger to learn. Mack would insist that Meyer sit beside him on the bench to discuss the various game situations. Meyer was learning the art of managing from one of the greatest ever in Connie Mack. Mack recognized Meyer as a marginal player on the field but he saw in Meyer a keen and astute student of the game. Managerial material to be certain.

It was very apparent to Meyer that his days as a player were waning and, with a passion for the game, he gave up his catching gear for a lineup card and began his journey traveling the minor league circuit earning his managerial stripes at the lowest of levels. In 1932 Meyer joined the New York Yankees organization and would eventually manage the Yankees highest farm clubs at Oakland, Newark and Kansas City. Joe McCarthy was enjoying a strong run in New York winning eight pennants from 1931 to 1946 until ill health forced him out of the dugout early in 1946. The natural successor appeared to be Meyer, but Meyer himself was battling ulcers and he was counseled by his physician not to take the position simply because his ulcers could not stand the pressure of the job. Instead, the Yankees named Bill Dickey manager. Dickey would not last the year, eventually handing over the reins to Johnny Neun late in the season.

In 1947 the Pirates were last in the National League at 62-92 under manager Billy Herman. The Pirates' front office had little patience with Herman and decided a change was in order. Meanwhile, Meyer's ulcers seemed to be under control and he was being hailed as a minor league manager whose time had come to make the leap into the big leagues. In 1948 the Pittsburgh Pirates made Meyer an offer to manage the club. This was Meyer's chance for a big league job and he didn't blink before saying yes. The years of riding worn out buses and playing baseball on diamonds with dirt infields and chicken wire backstops finally paid off.

In 1948, under Meyer, the Pirates finished fourth in the National League with a record of 83-71 and the easy going Tennessean from Knoxville was named Manager of the Year. But the honeymoon was short-lived, as the Pirates followed 1948 with records of 71-83, 57-96 and 64-90 over the next three seasons. Then came 1952. No one, not even Meyer, could have envisioned just how bad the Pirates would perform in what would be his final season in the dugout.

As the Pirates opened spring training camp at Perris Hill Park in San Bernardino California, Meyer was often reminded that his squad was comprised of the same players who had lost 96 and 90 games the previous two years. When asked what his starting lineup might look like on opening day a month away, Meyer could only say for sure that three of his starters would be Ralph Kiner in left field, Gus Bell in right and Jack Merson at second base. Kiner, a six-year veteran, had hit .309 in 1951 with a league leading 42

7

home runs and 109 runs batted in. Bell exhibited power hitting 16 home runs in 600 at bats with a .278 batting average. Merson had a late season promotion from the minors in '51 hitting .360 in 13 games and had sure hands at second base. After that, filling out the lineup card was a matter of pulling names out of a hat.

Jack Phillips, who hit .237 with no home runs in 156 at bats in 1951, was thrown into a mix at first base with George Metkovich (.293, 3HR), rookie Tony Bartirome, and Dick Hall, a 6-foot-6 stringbean rookie out of Swathmore College who had never played one inning of professional baseball. Bartirome, a slick-fielding 18-year-old native of Pittsburgh, would win the first base starting position. Bartirome would end up hitting .220 in 1952 with no home runs in 355 at bats in what would be his one and only fling as a major league player. Bartirome, who set a record by not hitting into a double play all season, went into the army in 1953 and his career as a player was over. However, Bartirome came back to the Pirates in 1967 as the team trainer and kept that position before retiring in 1985. Phillips, despite being the favorite early in the spring, would appear in only one game.

George Strickland (.216) was the starting shortstop in '51, but 5-foot-6 rookie Clem Koshorek would beat out the veteran in spring training. Koshorek held the position until the Pirates signed Dick Groat out of Duke University later in the season. Pete Castiglione (.261) had only seven home runs in 482 at bats as a starter at third in 1951 so rookie Lee Walls was being touted as a possible replacement. But it was Hall who got the call on opening day only to lose the job after three games. Meyer then went with Castiglione who would be just one of ten Pirates to play the hot corner in '52.

Since he was beat out at first base by Bartirome, it was assumed Metkovich would be back in center but Bobby Del Greco, a fleet rookie from Pittsburgh, had a good spring and won the starting job. Meyer stood by Del Greco, who ended up hitting just .217 in 341 at bats. Clyde McCullough (.297) and Joe Garagiola (.255) shared catching duties in '51 and both would return in 1952.

As for the pitching staff, Murry Dickson won 20 games in 1951 (20-16, 4.02 ERA) and was expected to lead the starting rotation followed by Howie Pollet (6-10, 5.04 ERA) and Bob Friend (6-10, 4.27 ERA). Vern Law was 6-9 (4.50 ERA) as a starter in 1951 but he would be lost to the Pirates while serving a two-year stint in the Army. The remainder of the staff would be comprised of Forrest Main, Ted Wilks, Paul LaPalme, Cal Hogue, Jim Waugh, Bill Werle and Ron Kline. Hardly a staff to put fear into the likes of the Brooklyn Dodgers and New York Giants.

It may have been the ulcers or it may have been the constant losing or a combination of both, but Meyer's personality turned callous as he transformed into more of a no non-sense guy. A glimpse of the new Meyer surfaced as the Pirates were barnstorming from California by way of Texas after spring training. Werle, a left-hander who was 8-6 in 1951 and expected to give the pitching staff some depth, was fined $500 by Meyer and suspended for what was deemed as breaking training rules. Werle was soon placed on waivers.

Meyer made his position clear: "This is only the beginning. I will not tolerate any more violation of training rules. I'm through covering up. This year is going to be different. The players are going to do things my way or they will do it their way - on some other club. I've gone to bat with Mr. (Branch) Rickey (general manager) for several players on this club and Werle was one of them. And I don't intend going again for anyone. Mr. Rickey gave me full authority to hand out whatever discipline I see fit and by golly I'm going to do it."

The Pirates finished the exhibition season with an 11-15 record, including one tie, and plenty of question marks. Actually, the won-loss record was not indicative of how bad the Pirates really were. With the 1952 opener looming in St. Louis against the Cardinals, the Pirates would be taking a roster weighed down with 13 rookies, including four players still in their teens. The youth movement was in full swing.

Pittsburgh had been one of the more successful and consistent teams in the National League over the past half-century. Under the ownership of Barney Dreyfuss (1900-31) the Pirates had six first-place finishes and seven second- and third-places finishes. After Dreyfuss passed away in 1932 his son-in-law, Bill Benswanger, assumed operation of the club and from 1932 to 1946 the Pirates never finished first but had four second-place finishes and only four second division finishes. One of those second division finishes was 1946 when the Pirates came in seventh.

In 1947 the family-owned Pirates was sold for $2.5 million to John Galbreath, Tom Johnson, Fred McKinney and singer Bing Crosby. The new ownership watched their investment bomb. After finishing 57-96 in 1950 and in eighth place, 331/2 games out of first, the owners went after Branch Rickey, who had severed his relations with Brooklyn after the 1950 season.

The owners appeared to have absolute confidence that Rickey could and would rebuild the Pirates franchise into a solid organization just as he had done in St. Louis and Brooklyn. Rickey took the challenge and truly believed he could transform the Pirates into a winning club. In 1951 Rickey convinced the owners that the key to success was turning around the Pirates' weak farm system and the only way to get this done was by pouring money, lots of money, into the plan. The owners assured themselves that Rickey would build a farm system for Pittsburgh mirroring those he had so successfully left behind in St. Louis and Brooklyn. In 1951 Rickey doled out $600,000 in signing several hundred young prospects to fill the rosters of the Pirates' 15 minor league affiliates. Those youngsters were part of a long-range plan and were of no help to the current club.

The Pirates struggled miserably at the start of the 1952 season with a 3-12 record, including a 10-game losing streak, for the month of April and began May with a six-game losing streak. The season was basically over at that point. With the turnstiles at Forbes Field rusting due to lack of use, rumors surfaced of Meyer being on the way out. But Rickey was sticking with Meyer and periodically would give his manager a vote of confidence.

Garagiola, who in later years would be better known for his broadcasting than he was for his professional career as a catcher, offered a lighthearted view of that horrible Pirates' team: "We had 154 games on our schedule and we showed up for every game. We lost eight of our first nine games and then we went into a slump. The 1952 Pirates were probably the only team in baseball history that clinched last place on opening day of spring training."

For the first month of the '52 season a power shortage existed as the three big guns that were expected to ignite the Pirates were struggling. Kiner bashed a home run in the opening game but zero over the next 14. Merson owned two home runs and Bell, who hit 16 in 1951, was at Triple-A Hollywood. Bell was demoted to Hollywood after hitting only .056 in seven games and was tagged by the Pirates brass as having a bad attitude detrimental to the team.

Bell returned to Pittsburgh in the middle of May with the expectations of supporting Kiner who had fallen into a deep slump. Kiner had only two home runs and nine runs batted in while hitting .220. When Bell, who hit behind Kiner in the lineup in the number five slot, left the team Kiner was hitting .458 with 11 hits in 24 at bats. After Bell's demotion Kiner had only seven hits in 58 at bats for a .121 average. Only days after Bell arrived there was more bad news for the Pirates as Kiner began suffering from back and leg ailments.

As Memorial Day came the Pirates were entrenched in last place in the National League at 8-32 and 20 1/2 games behind the Dodgers. For Meyer, the losses were bringing back memories of the 1916 Philadelphia A's club he was on that dropped a record-setting 117 games. The negative stories appearing daily in the local papers took a back seat to some good news for a change with the signing of Pittsburgh native and Duke All-America basketball player Dick Groat who was quickly inserted into the lineup at shortstop.

While a great addition to the club, no one was expecting Groat to turn the Pirates' season around by himself in the second half. The pitching staff was taking a beating as Dickson, who won 20 in 1951, was headed for 20 defeats, as he was 5-12 on July 4. "I don't see how I can miss," Dickson said of losing 20. "I've got 12 defeats now and prospects don't look much brighter."

With Kiner mired in a slump, the roster down to 20 players due to injuries and a pitching staff without an ounce of confidence as the Pirates lost 18 games after the sixth inning in games they were leading, there was little reason to be optimistic about the second half of the season. Rickey personally toured the minor league system looking for any immediate help but came back to Pittsburgh empty handed. Other than some young pitching prospects the cupboard was bare. By this point in the season fresh arms would have been welcome, especially by Wilks who, by the Pirates' 82nd game, had warmed up in the bullpen 61 times.

It seemed nothing was going right for the Pirates. Late in July Castiglione suffered a fractured right arm when hit by a pitch from Philadelphia's Andy Hansen. Umpire Tom Gorman ruled the ball hit Castiglione's bat on what was a bunt attempt and he called Castiglione out to end the game as the Pirate batter lay moaning in the dirt at home plate. Only a few days later Kiner was benched with a recurring back injury resulting from a pinched nerve.

With a cast constantly changing and with losses mounting at an alarming rate, Meyer addressed his club: "You clowns can go on *What's My Line* in uniform and stump the panel."

Garagiola had his own take on the '52 Pirates: "We gave the fans their money's worth. They always saw the bottom of the ninth. We'd be a couple of runs down before the National Anthem was over. People would leave after Kiner batted for the last time and walk across the field - while we were still on it."

Friend, who would end his career with the Yankees and Mets in 1966 with a career record of 197-230 and an ERA of 3.58, is honest in his assessment of the '52 Pirates: "We didn't have a club that could compete. They brought up young kids too quickly. But their reasoning was to get the young kids experience and they'd help us down the road. I know we would go into a town and you'd hear the fans yelling 'Here come the cellar dwellers.'"

Del Greco was one of those young players brought up early: "Rickey just brought up too many too soon. There were several

18- and 19-year-old kids, including myself. Rickey figured if he was going to lose, he might as well lose with the younger players. We had a bad ball club. I know it hurt me personally coming up too fast. I didn't adapt to major league pitching. But I wanted to come up. You're a young kid and they're going to bring you up to the major leagues, you're not going to say no. If I had stayed down the whole year in the minors it might have helped me."

Rickey realized the young guys weren't ready for big league ball. More seasoning in the minors was the preferable alternative but the Pirates needed help. Rickey had to take a chance with the youngsters.

"If I had a going ball club now, none of them would be with us," Rickey was quoted in the *Pittsburgh Sun-Telegraph*. "They'd all be in the farm system absorbing experience. But we're doing a force-feeding job. We're trying to rush things because we're in a fix and have to do it."

The force-feeding just wasn't working. The young kids were being overmatched. As a matter of fact, it was rare that any of the rookies played at home. "I am going to play the kids once we get on the road," Meyer said. "Right now, the way we are going, I am afraid the fans will break their morale. The club is going badly and they might start getting on the youngsters. That could ruin them for the season. We can't expect miracles. I still believe in the kids and I am going down the line with them. We have to stick with them."

While the roster was filled with untested youngsters, there were other young players who were toiling in the minors waiting for their chance at the majors. One such youngster was Ronald Necciai, a 19-year-old right-hander from Monongahela, Pennslyvania, a small town 30 miles south of Pittsburgh. Necciai was to have made the trip to Pittsburgh out of spring training but recurring ulcers prevented him from making the 25-man roster. Necciai was farmed out but he would eventually get the call late in the season. While the Pirates were struggling through the early months of 1952, Necciai's name kept appearing in the local Pittsburgh papers as the young phenom was turning in some rather impressive numbers at the Pirates' Class D farm club.

The front office was tempted to catapult Necciai up the ladder but Rickey felt patience would be in the best interest for the young pitcher. Rickey wanted to make sure Necciai's ulcers were manageable and the timing was right to break Necciai in. As for the Pittsburgh fans, everything they had been reading in the papers indicated the next Bob Feller was coming to Forbes Field. The fans were primed to see this hard throwing kid on the mound in Forbes. And so was the front office as local boy makes good means more clicks at the turnstiles. It would be just a matter of time.

Chapter 2

Young Ron

Each morning during the school year, young Ron Necciai made the ten minute trek from the family home just off Rainbow Run Road to Sunnyside Grade School in Gallatin, Pennsylvania, a small burg of about 350 people situated across the Monongahela River from the town of Monongahela. The winter months in western Pennslyvania can be brutally cold and the wind whipping off the river often chilling to the bone.

Anna, Ron's mother, was a petite and soft-spoken woman. She would send the third of her four children out the door of their modest home wrapped in a warm overcoat with books cradled under one arm clutching in his free hand a brown paper sack containing the day's lunch, usually consisting of a sandwich and an apple. There would be some days when Ron would not see his mother at all before leaving home for school. After Anna's husband, Attilio, died in 1937 from a bout with pneumonia, she would find various jobs cleaning houses to support the family which, in addition to Ron, included older siblings Violet and Attilio junior and Sandra, who was three years younger than Ron.

As Ron trudged along the road, gray plumes of smoke spiraled into the sky from the many steel mills and coke plants lining the Monongahela River all the way to Pittsburgh, 30 miles to the north. It was virtually impossible to distinguish where one mill stopped and another began. The smoke from the mills seemed to always hover over the Monongahela Valley covering houses with its black and grimy soot and discoloring what once were white clapboard homes into gray dwellings. The smoke and soot, as well as the rancid smell that permeated the air, was part of the landscape. For those who lived and worked here, the polluted air meant jobs and jobs meant food on the table. Working the mills in the mid-1940s was the livelihood of thousands just as it was a generation before and a generation before that. The mills were the means by which a family survived in this part of the country.

The senior Attilio labored at the Combustion Mill and when Ron was old enough he, too, would no doubt be working those very same mills. It was the natural sequence for sons to follow their fathers. Ron was only five when Attilio died. The younger Necciai had only vague memories of his father but, from stories Anna would tell Ron, it was clear he had a loving father. She would tell how Attilio would come home after working a long shift and ride Ron around the house on his back. Life was short for Attilio and he left behind a young family without a means of support. No matter how tough times may have been, Anna made sure to shower her children with love and the children adjusted to life without a father.

After the elder Attilio died, the Necciai family became dependent upon one another with Violet and Attilio Jr. entrusted with looking after the younger siblings. Anna was forced to provide for the family making a difficult transition from housewife to that of a single working mother. It wasn't easy paying the bills and putting

17

Anna and Attilio Necciai hold Ron's sister Sandra in 1936. (Courtesy Ron Necciai).

food on the table. As a matter of fact, sometimes it seemed almost impossible.

So when the children reached their teen years they each found work to earn money taking on odd jobs around the valley. Work, however, did not and would not interfere with school. Seeing that each of her children received the proper education was a priority for Anna. She and Attilio had dreams for their kids. They both wanted a better life for their children and a better life was anything but toiling in the mills. A college education appeared to be the only means by which they could escape the mills and live out their own dreams.

As far as Ron was concerned, school was just a necessary evil. He did not enjoy the daily grind of going to class. At the same time, he understood that he must apply himself and do the best work that he could in school. Anna would make sure that Ron, and all of her children, did their homework each night and studied for upcoming tests. A report card with Cs was not acceptable. Ron was a good student but it was while attending Sunnyside that Ron discovered baseball - a pastime that would interest him much more than books.

"Lewis Warren was the headmaster of the school system and he organized baseball teams for the five elementary schools so that they could play against one another," Necciai recalls. "I was on the team at Sunnyside and that's how I got started playing baseball. I was probably about 11 or 12 years old."

Ron was hooked. From the elementary school diamonds Necciai began playing in the booster league for kids during the summer months. Little League was formed in 1939 but had not yet been established in Necciai's backyard.

"There were several teams in the area," Necciai says. "We didn't have uniforms. We just played in our old clothes. Maybe two guys on our team had spikes. Not every kid had a glove. When you came in from playing defense, you left your glove on the field just in case a kid on the other team didn't have one. From the time I got up in the morning all I could think about was getting over to the field to play baseball."

When he was 12, young Ron began caddying at the Monongahela Valley Country Club after school and during the summer months. Nevertheless, he always found time for baseball and as Ron grew older it was apparent he had a rare talent for the game. Ron advanced from the booster league to the valley league.

"The valley league was an amateur league for men," Necciai says. "It was mainly for guys just out of high school on up to guys who were in their 40s. I was about 16 and Harry Sickles, who was the coach, asked me to play. I pitched a little bit but mostly I played first base. I was a pretty good hitter back then. In the summer I would play American Legion ball."

As Ron's elementary school years were ending and his high school days beginning, he had grown into a tall and lanky stringbean of a teen-ager and quite athletic. Gallatin had no high school so Necciai had to choose between high schools in nearby Monessen, Elizabeth, Monongahela or Donora. He chose Monessen because of the persistence of the high school football coach who called and visited Ron at every opportunity. The coach had seen Ron play soccer and was impressed with his ability to kick. Monessen was about 30 minutes from Gallatin and after attending a month Necciai decided to leave and transfer to Monongahela High School, now Ringgold High, which was closer to home. Necciai had played a little soccer and had developed a kicking style catching the attention of Monongahela's football coach, just as he had caught the eye of the Monessen coach.

"Ben Haldy, the football coach at Monongahela, said that I would be good at kicking extra points and field goals. But he said he was going to have to teach me to kick with my toe and not soccer style. Of course, today, they all kick soccer style," says Necciai, who also had the right build and the good hands to play the tight end position. "Alex DeRosa was the punter and kickoff man and Coach Haldy wanted someone to take some of the pressure off Alex so that's why he had me kicking the field goals and extra points."

Ron (right) with brother Attilio and sister Violet in 1937. (Courtesy Ron Necciai).

There was one problem with football. Anna was leary of her son playing a game where he could end up breaking a leg.

"My mother was my hero and she supported me in everything I wanted to do - except football," Necciai recalls. "She didn't like football one bit. It was just too rough for her and I don't think she really understood the game entirely. But when I went out for football and made the team my sophomore year she didn't even know I was playing. When I was late coming home after practice or gone to games on Friday night she thought I was working or hanging out with my friends. I might have somehow given her that impression.

"Nobody ever told her I was playing and she never went to the games. Had no reason to. In 1949 our last home game was against Monessen. It was on Armistice Day. It was my mother's birthday and she decided to go to the game just to watch the halftime activities. I had no idea she was coming. She just showed up. Well, she was there and they announced my name. That was the first time she ever knew I was playing. She really scolded me good."

Necciai was very talented in three sports - baseball, football and soccer. Being almost six feet tall in high school the one game in which he would seem a natural was basketball.

"When I went to high school I had never played basketball," Necciai says. "I was taking a hygiene class and the teacher was Moe Johnson who was also the basketball coach. He asked me to play. I told him I really wasn't interested. I was walking down the hall to class one day and he stopped me and said instead of coming to class for me to go to the gym and shoots some hoops. Kids always look for the chance to skip class so I went to the gym. I later went out for the team and made it. I was very uncoordinated, as I had just started shooting up in height. Playing basketball really helped me in gaining my coordination."

As the seasons changed, so would Necciai from football to basketball to baseball and soccer.

Necciai, like many of his friends, was looking ahead to the day when he would graduate high school. While his mother was still talking to him about college, Ron was being more realistic and was convinced he would be working in the local mill, as the money wasn't available for a college education. There was the outside chance that maybe he could obtain an athletic scholarship as college scouts had been to Monongahela's football and baseball

The 1950 Monongahela High School baseball team with Ron Necciai in the middle row, third from the left. (Courtesy Ron Necciai).

games and it was obvious they had more than just a casual interest in Necciai.

Baseball was Necciai's first love and what would be better than to get a free college education and play baseball. By the time Necciai entered his senior year in high school, word was spreading across western Pennsylvania about this Necciai kid who could hit a ton. And Necciai could throw bullets but he seldom got the chance to do that from the mound.

"I played first base and Coach Haldy one day asked me to try pitching," Necciai recalls. "I could throw pretty hard but I didn't know where the ball was going and neither did anybody else. My first couple games that I pitched I hit several batters. It got to the point everybody was bailing out. After I hit a couple of guys in a row in one game Coach Haldy said he was moving me back to first base permanently before I killed somebody. I still got to pitch some but I was the third guy on the staff and used mainly to mop up."

While growing up Necciai's closest friend was Alex DeRosa. They were classmates at Sunnyside Grade School and graduated together from Monongahela High. DeRosa, like Necciai, was active in athletics just about the whole year round. DeRosa was a fullback and kicker in football and a catcher on the baseball squad.

"When we were growing up, playing sports was all we did," DeRosa says. "Ron and I were always close. We didn't live that far apart in Gallatin. We'd walk to school together. Ron had a little further walk than I did as he lived about five blocks further up the road. We played sports together. Football and baseball and sandlot and the American Legion ball. We were typical high school kids. We were best friends. We never got in trouble because we didn't have time to. We were always playing sports, night and day. Ron was a heckuva athlete. He was the end on our football team. A tall end. He was a very, very good baseball player. He played first base but he could throw. Had a fastball and curve but everyone was afraid of him because he was so wild. You could see that Ron had a future in baseball."

DeRosa wasn't such a bad athlete himself. Supporting a solid 184 pounds on a 5-foot-101/2 inch frame, DeRosa was a hardnosed fullback and a pretty good catcher and could hit the ball a country mile. As a senior at Monongahela, DeRosa was courted by a number of college and university football recruiters.

After their high school graduation, DeRosa and Necciai both received letters dated June 5 from the Pittsburgh Pirates inviting the close friends to Forbes Field for a tryout on June 13. The story circulating was that Tony Rockino, a barber who cut hair of some of the Pirates at the Schenley Hotel in Pittsburgh, was responsible for suggesting the Pirates give the pair a look. Necciai to this day says he never saw or spoke or even knew Rockino. However,

Frank Pizzica, an auto dealer in Monongahela, apparently had called the Pirates several times suggesting the Pirates might want to check out both DeRosa and Necciai. Also throwing around the names of Necciai and DeRosa were Haldy, Sickles and Jerome Brody, manager of the Junior Legion Monongahela Unionmen. Whoever may have been responsible for getting the Pirates' attention, the end result was the invitation to try out.

Necciai was doing general labor at the Liggett Spring and Axle plant making a dollar an hour at the plant which was less than a mile from his new home in Manown, where the family moved before his senior year. Necciai would walk from Manown, which was about a mile west of Gallatin, to his job five days a week doing general clean up. Necciai had no career in mind and really wasn't thinking about baseball. His high school baseball career was over and, he assumed, so was his baseball career in general. Then came the Pirates' invitation.

"I thought it might be fun," Necciai says. "Never really thought much about signing. I was working after school in the plant where they made springs and axles for Willis Overland Jeep. Pretty boring job. And it was dirty and greasy in that plant. Each day you'd come out covered in dirt. For some of the guys there it was the only life they knew. They'd work those mills for 50 years. But I thought going to the tryout was a good excuse to get me out of the mill for a day. I worked out and hit a couple of balls and this guy comes over and wanted to know if I wanted to go and play pro ball. He offered me $150 a month. Right then I thought, 'Boy, I hate working in that mill.' My idea of life wasn't working in the mill for the rest of my life. I was only 17."

DeRosa was exploring all of his options which also included a free ride to several colleges to play football. During that era, an athlete who signed a pro contract in any sport could not play collegiately in another. And, too, DeRosa's father was encouraging his son to go to college but the younger DeRosa was intent on playing pro baseball. When the Pirates did not offer a signing bonus, DeRosa felt certain that another team would come through with some extra money. So, he turned the Pirates down. A few weeks later, the New York Giants called, offered a modest incentive and DeRosa signed on the dotted line.

DeRosa played two years in the minor leagues before being drafted into the United States Army. After spending 18 months in France, DeRosa received an honorable discharge. The desire to play pro ball was still there but the talent had eroded. After a couple of failed tryouts, DeRosa, now married with a child, went back to Monongahela and went to work in the mills. "It wasn't meant to be," says DeRosa. "Back then I thought I could make it. But I knew Ronnie could make it. Right after we graduated I told Ronnie to get away from here and go play ball. I caught him enough to know he had it. Man he had it. I remember telling Ronnie not to throw his arm away. I tried to warn him. He could have made it if he had taken care of himself."

Meanwhile, a couple of days later Charlie Muse, who was the inventor of the hard hat used by hitters and a Pittsburgh scout, went to the Necciai house to speak with Ron's mother and step-father, Andrew Michlik, who Anna had been married to for about a year. Muse wanted Necciai and Necciai definitely wanted to sign a contract but nothing would happen until Ron's step-father and mother agreed to put their signatures on the contract, since Ron was a minor. Anna still had dreams of Ron going to college but Ron's dreams had changed. After a few minutes discussing the situation and seeing how much Ron wanted to give professional baseball a try, the deal was consummated. "Mother and my step-father were for whatever I wanted to do. So I signed with the Pirates," Necciai says.

There was no bonus for Ron although the Pirates were dishing out modest bonuses to other signees. All Ron had was a promise of $150 a month, a bus ticket and the chance to play baseball. It sounded like the perfect deal and a free pass out of the mill.

Chapter 3

Escaping the Mills

Necciai, at 17, was more than ready to escape the smoldering smokestacks of western Pennsylvania. The world beckons at such a young age and the stretch of real estate along the Monongahela River with its ever present billowing gray plumes was as far as Necciai ever ventured. A man's life was measured by how many years he worked in the mills before retiring and Necciai had seen men grow old before their time. He wanted more out of life than the daily grind of the mills.

Necciai possessed a talent for playing baseball and now this special gift might just be his ticket to leaving forever the drudgery of the 7-to-3 shift. It was not uncommon to read in the paper where some kid from this part of the state of Pennsylvania had signed to play professional baseball and it was not uncommon to never hear from that kid again. For every Stan Musial, who was from nearby Donora, there were hundreds of young men through the years who signed with every expectation of starring in the big leagues only to have their dreams fizzle. Necciai never considered himself as having the extraordinary talent to play in the majors. He realized the odds were against him ever reaching that level. At the same time, Necciai believed he could play minor league ball a couple of years, make a little money and have some fun. When the time came to hang up his glove, then he would go on with the rest of his life.

While Necciai's ability to play baseball came natural as a kid, he now had to learn how to play the game above the level to which he had been accustomed in high school and on the sandlots around Monongahela. He had been advised to pay attention to his coaches in the minor leagues as they all had experienced the growing pains of playing professional baseball. Listen and learn he was instructed. The wisdom to be passed down was from men who had dedicated their lives to baseball.

Necciai never heard of the North Carolina State League. For that matter he never heard of Salisbury, North Carolina where he was to report to begin his professional baseball career. Salisbury was a town of about 15,000 located in the Piedmont area of the state with Winston-Salem 40 miles to the north and Charlotte 40 miles to the south and endless fields of tobacco in between.

North Carolina was a state rich in minor league baseball history. During much of the 1940s and 1950s it seemed as if every city and town in North Carolina, no matter how large or how small, had some level of minor league baseball. Salisbury was one of those towns. Even going back to the days of the Civil War baseball was quite popular. A Confederate prison holding Union soldiers was located near Salisbury and history documents that those Union soldiers played baseball nearly every day. Toward the end of the 19th century town teams were formed and soon to follow were industrial and textile leagues. Baseball was an integral part of life. The town of Salisbury, in 1937, would field a professional team in the North Carolina State League and would remain a member of the league until the league folded after the 1952 season.

Necciai had little idea as to what to expect upon reporting to Salisbury. When Necciai signed his contract with the Pirates it was, he assumed, as a first baseman. Why would he even think otherwise? First base was his position throughout his high school career and he developed into a sure handed fielder and he could hit. So, it only seemed logical that he would be given a first baseman's mitt when he reported for duty in Salisbury. The Pirates had other plans for Necciai.

The manager at Salisbury was George Detore (Dee-tore) - a career minor league player and manager. During the early spring of 1950 Necciai and Detore barely said hello before saying goodbye. For the brief time Necciai was at Salisbury, he never wore a first baseman's mitt. Instead, the Pirates had already decided the youngster, who possessed a cannon for an arm, would pitch. Necciai was an above average hitter in high school, but Pirate scouts predicted that once the curveballs began breaking, his career would take a nosedive. So many young ballplayers feast as amateurs on fastballs only to discover the frustration of being frozen at the plate by sharp breaking curveballs.

"When I signed I thought all the time it was as a first baseman," Necciai recalls. "But the first day there Detore took me aside and told me to forget about playing first base that I was going to pitch. I was surprised because I never had pitched that much in high school. It didn't matter to me what they wanted to do. I just wanted to play. As for pitching, all I could do was throw hard. I had no control and no breaking pitch."

Necciai's tenure on the Salisbury roster was just long enough to pitch three innings over a two-game span. In those three innings he allowed four hits, seven runs and six bases on balls without striking out a single batter. The Salisbury roster was over its 17-player limit so the Pirates transferred Necciai to Shelby, North Carolina of the Class D West Carolina League. It proved to be an unpopular move for Necciai.

Shelby was, much like Salisbury, a small town situated between Asheville and Charlotte. The change in scenery wasn't a boost to Necciai's career or his morale. Necciai appeared in one game giving up one hit, three runs and two walks.

"As soon as I reported to the Shelby team we were on the road at Lincolnton," Necciai recalls. "We were there for two days and I thought, 'This isn't for me.' So I quit. My baseball career, as far as I was concerned, was over at that point. I was impulsive and still am sometimes. I thought I lived in the dump of the world with all the mills back home but when we went to Lincolnton I thought that place was even worse. This was not my idea of where I wanted to be. And I was getting rocked. I wasn't a pitcher. I had no confidence. I thought to myself I wasn't going to make any money like this."

Necciai packed his bags, returned home to Monongahela and immediately went back to work at Liggett Spring and Axle. As the summer months dragged on and as Necciai each day faced clocking in at the mill, he could not imagine spending the rest of his working life at this mundane and low paying job.

"The longer I was working in that mill the more I made up my mind that this isn't for me either," Necciai says. "I got home one afternoon and my brother Til was there. I remember telling Til that I'm done. I'm never going back to those mills. I didn't know what I was going to do but I'm not going back ever again to the mills. I'd do anything but work in the mills."

Meanwhile, the Pirates had not given up on Necciai. It was not uncommon for young players to get their confidence shattered early in their pro careers and come back and be productive. The Pirates still felt Necciai had the ability to develop as a pitcher if he would just give it a try. Pirates' scout Charlie Muse visited Necciai at home several times, attempting to convince Ron to come back and play ball. Muse pointed out to Necciai that there was no future for him in the mills, as if he needed to be told. Muse stressed to Necciai that there was a bright future for him in baseball if only he would give the game another try.

"Charlie said I ought to give it a go," Necciai remembers. "Charlie told me I shouldn't give up. He pointed out that this was a once in a lifetime opportunity and that I shouldn't throw it away. And I had a couple of friends who were telling me the same thing. They were saying don't give up and I should go back to baseball. I talked with Muse a few more times and over the winter I thought about it more and decided that I would go to spring training and see what happens. I really didn't have much to lose."

The green baseball diamonds and the warm weather at the Pirates training facility in Deland, Florida were more to Necciai's liking than the snow that covered the ground back home. Necciai was soaking up the sun and confident he had made the right decision to give baseball another shot. Even though Muse had given Necciai so many pep talks about how he was a sure bet to make the grade in pro ball, Necciai wasn't buying the hype. Necciai, lacking confidence after his less than successful introduction to the game, found it hard to believe that he had what it took to be legitimate prospect. He failed to see what the Pirates saw in him but if the Pirates were willing to have him back what did he have to lose? At least he wouldn't be sweating his life away in the mills.

At the minor league camp, Necciai would throw from the mound on a daily basis and word spread quickly about this lanky, hard-throwing 18-year-old. The kid threw bullets but hitting his target was the adventure. No one, not even Necciai, had any idea as to where the ball would end up once it left his hand. Ten feet in front of the plate, high over the catcher and against the backstop or flush into the batter's ribs. Everyone was convinced that once he learned how to get the ball across the plate, Necciai would write his own ticket to Pittsburgh.

With lots of work and instruction, it was just a matter of time that Necciai would eventually find his control. At least that's what the baseball experts were saying. And no one believed that more than George Detore. It was Detore's faith in Necciai that would carry the young right-hander through many ups-and-downs. Detore was the type of manager who could instill confidence in the most downtrodden young player. Detore was part manager, part psychologist and a whole lot Svengali.

Detore, born George Francis Detore in Utica, New York in 1906, was a man of small stature standing only 5-foot-8 but weighing a stout 170 pounds. Detore radiated an authoritative presence. Throughout his playing career in the minor leagues, with a brief stint in the majors, it was apparent to other baseball people that Detore could make a career of the game as a coach or manager. Detore was signed by Cleveland in 1929 after excelling for three years at Colgate University, and played his first pro season at shortstop in Decatur, Illinois. In 1930 he was promoted to New Orleans, had a good year and at the end of the season was brought up to Cleveland where he started three games at third base. The 1931 season was a repeat of 1930 with a little more playing time with the Indians getting into 30 games playing third, short and second base and hitting a respectable .268. In 1932 Detore was optioned to Buffalo. It was while playing for Buffalo that Detore had one remarkable game as he went six-for-six (three singles, three home runs) and scored six runs, all in a six inning game. Detore was sold to Toledo in 1933 and then to Milwaukee in 1934 remaining there through 1936. In 1937 Detore suited up in San Diego and stayed with the club through 1944 serving as a player-manager the last two years. He won the PCL batting title in 1937 and was second six times.

Detore's final season as an active player was 1945 as a player-coach with Indianapolis. But his wayfaring days in the minor leagues were not close to being over. In 1946 he was back with Toledo as a coach and then as manager. In 1947 he managed Williamsport in the Eastern League and returned to Toledo as manager in 1948 and it was back to Milwaukee in 1949 as a coach. Detore would join the Pittsburgh organization in 1950 as manager at Salisbury winning the North Carolina State League pennant.

"George was a mighty good man," Necciai says affectionately of Detore, who he calls his mentor. "George was probably the most patient man I've ever been around. To say he was a great help to me would be an understatement."

The two barely got to know one another when Necciai first reported to Salisbury in 1950 but that would change as Necciai was reunited with Detore in Salisbury in 1951. A bond quickly formed. A bond that put Detore in the position of a father that Necciai never knew. Detore earned a respect from Necciai that would last a lifetime.

Detore had a quiet demeanor. It was rare Detore would raise his voice. It was even more rare that he would berate a player. If anything needed to be conveyed between manager and player, it was handled privately behind closed doors. Detore was a teacher and his students listened. He was managing Salisbury for the second straight season when Necciai arrived on the scene.

The first day at Salisbury Detore grabbed a catcher's mitt in the dugout and pointed Necciai in the direction of the mound. Detore squatted behind the plate and instructed Necciai to fire away. Necciai wound up and delivered a pitch that wouldn't have broken a pane of glass.

"Hey, you're warmed up aren't ya?" Detore asked.

"Yeah, Mr. Detore. I'm warmed up."

Detore squatted down again and held up the target. Necciai wound up and again threw a fastball making a soft thud as it hit the leather mitt.

"Hey, can't you throw harder than that?" Detore bellowed.

"I guess," Necciai answered.

"Well, throw the dang ball then," Detore said as he went back behind the plate.

Necciai came off the mound and motioned for Detore to meet him.

"Something wrong kid?" Detore asked.

"Well, I'm not sure I can throw harder. I mean I can throw harder but I'm not sure if I can," an apologetic Necciai said with his eyes looking at the ground and not at Detore.

"You're not making any sense kid," a confused Detore said.

"Well, back in high school I was pitching and I threw a pitch that broke the ribs of this batter. The coach took me out of the game and made me promise never to throw that hard again."

Detore put his hand on Necciai's shoulder in a fatherly manner: "Listen kid, this ain't high school. You're going to get paid good money to throw hard and those hitters are going to get paid to get out of the way. If they get hit, it's their fault. Now, get back on the mound and throw the hell out of that ball."

Necciai nodded and went back on the mound as Detore went back behind the plate. Necciai uncorked a pitch that sounded like a rifle shot as it hit Detore's mitt. Detore flinched, took off his mitt and looked down at his hand before looking back up to Necciai on the mound. "That's it kid. You've got it," Detore said flashing a wide grin. "Just keep throwing that way and you'll be in Pittsburgh before you know it."

While Necciai was attempting to harness his control, Detore was impressing upon Necciai that he couldn't get by very long with just a fastball. It didn't matter if that fastball was hitting speeds in the upper 90 miles per hour. Any pitcher, even Walter Johnson, had to have an offspeed pitch. Sure, Necciai would get by in the minor leagues but when the time came to pitch against major league hitters, they would sit and wait on the fastball and eventually they would catch on and it didn't matter how hard you might throw. Necciai had to learn to throw the curveball. Without a curveball to complement the hard fastball, Detore warned Necciai that he might as well go home.

"I have a funny arm," Necciai says. "I have what they call long joints. It was difficult for me to throw a curveball like most people. It's the way my bones are structured. I had trouble throwing sliders or cut fastballs. I had to turn my arm more and more which is hard on the elbow."

Detore told Necciai of a pitcher he coached at Toledo who had the same arm problem. He tried to throw a curve but because of his arm action the ball would drop. He felt Necciai could achieve the same results. Detore took on Necciai as his own special project. Every day at Salisbury, Detore and Necciai would arrive at the park several hours early. At first it was only a matter of 10 or 15 feet and Detore would have Necciai throw the ball with a twist of his arm but nice and easy. The days would go by and the distance that Necciai would throw the pitch would increase. After a couple of months Necciai was having success with his newly discovered curveball.

"Ron developed a curve that is a beauty," Detore said to reporters. "He brings the ball straight overhand and lets the ball roll off the ends of his first two fingers. Not one guy in a thousand can deliver a pitch like that but the ones who can have a ball that does things. Ron can do it."

While Necciai was improving as a pitcher, control continued to be a consistent problem.

"Anybody who ever caught me would tell you that I was terrible to catch," Necciai admits. "I was always behind in the count. I would throw a lot of curves that would bounce in front of the plate. If I could get the pitch over the plate, I could get the hitters out. George tried to get me to throw a change and I had trouble with that as well. I would hesitate on the change and the hitters could tell what was coming when I did that and they hit nothing but line drives. The trick to throwing the change was not to follow through. Throw as hard as you want but keep your foot on the rubber until the ball was gone. It got to the point to where I could do that without thinking. Thanks to George."

Necciai arrived in Salisbury with a natural overhand delivery. It was just the way he threw. No one ever instructed him on how to pitch, he just did whatever felt natural.

"When it comes to throwing the fastball, it is a God-given talent," Necciai says. "I didn't have much of a windup or motion. It was almost like I had no windup."

Once in Salisbury, Pirates general manager Branch Rickey observed Necciai during his minor league tour of Pittsburgh's various farm clubs and suggested to Detore that he attempt to work with Necciai on a sidearm delivery. With Necciai's tall 6-foot-3 frame and the way the ball shot from his right hand, he would be more intimidating coming sidearm, especially with the bad lights of the minor leagues. Necciai would have the batters bailing out.

Kenny Barbao, a native of Donora whose father was a foreman in the zinc works at U.S. Steel and who managed the zinc works baseball team and coached a teen-age Stan Musial, would become one of Necciai's closest friends as the two roomed together while at Salisbury.

Barbao had worked in the mills like Necciai and had played on the American Legion championship team in 1950, the same team Necciai had played on the year before. But the two never crossed paths until spring training. Like Necciai, Barbao was a multi-sports star. Barbao signed a football scholarship at Washington & Jefferson but discovered early that college wasn't where he wanted to be. Barbao had made the football team at W&J but decided after a month of school to go south to Florida and catch on with a minor league team. Barbao's American Legion team attracted several major league scouts and they all were clamoring to get his signature on a contract. Showing the most interest in Barbao were the Pirates. In February of 1951, after leaving W&J, Barbao traveled to Deland, Florida and to the Pirates spring camp. The Pirates offered Barbao a contract and a $1,000 signing bonus. Barbao signed and became a part of Rickey's stable of players.

"Truth be known, the only reason I got to play pro ball was because the Pirates wanted me to hold Ron's hand," laughs Barbao.

Actually, Barbao had a ton of talent and was a legitimate pitching prospect. He jumped to Class B Waco halfway through the 1951 season and was progressing in the system when his career was interrupted by the Korean conflict, where he served in the U.S. Army. Barbao came back from service, picked up where he left off but injured his arm during spring training in 1955. At Salisbury, Necciai and Barbao roomed together, shared their accomplishments and troubles and made memories together.

"Kenny had a lot to do with me staying in pro ball," Necciai says. "On our $150 a month salary we were usually out of money with a week or ten days to go before our next paycheck came around. Kenny's father would send him some money and Kenny would share it with me. We never went hungry because that money would buy us hamburgers and fries."

Barbao knew Necciai about as well as anyone could. Barbao witnessed firsthand the ups and the downs that Necciai experienced as a fledgling minor league pitcher.

"Ron was a worrier," Barbao says. "But he was a fun-loving guy. We had some good times together. It's a shame he ended up hurting his arm. The first time I saw him pitch was in spring training. I knew he could hit because everyone talked about Ron in American Legion the year before I began playing. But in spring training I saw him pitch and boy, could he throw. I thought to myself, 'I've never seen anybody throw like this.' I know at Salisbury he wasn't doing all that well until he went sidearm and that made all the difference in the world."

Like most pitchers, Barbao likes to throw in a story about his hitting and Barbao was one pitcher who could beat the ball to death with a bat.

"I hit pretty good for a pitcher," Barbao says. "At Salisbury there was a sign at the park that if you hit a ball over that sign you would win a suit of clothes. I hit a ball over that sign and won the suit. It was a $79.79 suit. We struck up a deal with the store that gave the suit where Ron and I each got a shirt, a pair of pants and a belt if one of us hit a home run.

"Ron could hit too. We were at Lexington and Ron crushed the ball right out of the park but Ron had stepped across the plate and the umpire called him out. Boy, we gave it to Ron for that one. Ron and I were both pretty good at hitting golf balls too. There wasn't a lot to do in Salisbury and there was a golf course there with a driving range and we went down one time and each got a bucket of balls. We were hitting those things about 300 yards over the fence and losing them into the woods. We got through and asked for another bucket of balls and the guy said, 'That's all for you guys. No more.'

"I hit off of Ron one time and that was when we went to Forbes Field for a workout. Ron was pitching batting practice and I stepped up to hit and hit one off the clock in left field. I still won't let him live that down.

"Ron and I were both fortunate to play for a guy like Detore. He was a great manager. Didn't make a lot of noise, he was the quiet type. But what a great baseball mind he had. But I know one time I hit a home run and it was a common practice that the home crowd would pass the hat and they'd give you the money. I was in the dugout and someone passed the money through the fence for me and Detore saw me take it and said I wasn't allowed to have it and took it away. About midway through the year I was sent to Waco. Before I left the Salisbury club, George called me into his office and pulled the thirty dollars out of his desk and gave it back."

Necciai, who hit .404 for Salisbury, can't help but smile when speaking of Barbao.

"We called Kenny 'Ferdinand the Bull' because he was of Spanish descent and boy did he have a temper," Necciai recalls. "He got ripped on the mound one time. Didn't make it out of the first inning. He goes back to the clubhouse and tears it apart."

There were times that Necciai felt like doing a little damage to the clubhouse himself.

In the second game of the season at Mooresville and in his first appearance, in relief, Necciai pitched two and two thirds innings and suffered the loss as he walked six and allowed six hits. Necciai also had a bases-loaded double to drive in three runs. Necciai got his first start of the season at Hickory but took the 8-1 loss despite going seven innings and giving up just five hits. He walked six and fanned 10. Necciai struggled so much the first month of the season that he was ready to walk away from baseball again.

"I told George I was quitting," Necciai remembers. "George told me to hold on and not be hasty. George said, 'You need to make money don't you?' I said, 'Sure.' George said, 'Well, I need a bus driver. How about you driving the team bus?' Our regular bus driver was a relief pitcher we had by the name of Chief Bennett who was a full-blooded Cherokee. He was in his 30s, was having arm problems and George was going to let him go.

"George had asked me if I knew how to drive a bus and I told him I could but I actually had no clue as to how to drive a bus. We had a 20-passenger GMC bus. The North Carolina State League was a travel league. It was rare we stayed overnight anywhere we went. George said he would give me the job of driving the bus at $100 a month. I thought that was a lot of money. The thing was I had to drive the bus to Lexington that very night.

"Right away I went back and got Barbao and I said, 'Come on Ferdinand, we're going down to the ballpark. This was like 10 o'clock in the morning. He asked what for? I said you're looking at the new bus driver for the Salisbury baseball team. Kenny looked at me kind of funny and said, 'You can't drive a bus.' I looked at Kenny straight in the eye and said, 'I know I can't and that's why we're going down to the field and you're going to help me learn.' Kenny said, 'I don't know how to drive a bus.' I said, 'Well, we'll learn together.'

"We played at the Catawba College field and that's where the bus was always parked. I look up Homer the business manager and George had already told him about me driving the bus and so I got the keys from Homer. So Kenny gets in the bus with me and we're driving around the lot and I get in a corner and had to back up. Well, I didn't know how to put the bus in reverse. Kenny says, 'How in the hell can you drive this thing if you can't put it in reverse Ronnie?' It took a while but we finally figured it out.

"Well, that afternoon everybody loads up on the bus and I'm behind the wheel and George is sitting in the seat right behind me. We approach this narrow bridge with iron sides and I didn't want to get too close to the sides so I steered toward the middle of the road and just as we were crossing the bridge a tractor trailer comes the other way. I just nicked that truck with the mirror on the bus. George, in his calm manner said, 'Ron, you're OK son. Just stay on your side of the road. Somehow we made it to Lexington."

Barbao recalls Necciai's bus driving exploits.

"We were coming back from a game at night at High Point-Thomasville," Barbao says. "Everyone on the bus, including Detore, was asleep. The bus was weaving a bit and I got up and noticed that Ron's head was jerking back and forth. He was having a tough time staying awake. The rest of the way back I stood right beside Ron to make sure he didn't get us all killed."

As his bus driving skills improved, so too did Necciai's pitching. Just in case things didn't pan out, he warned his mother back home.

"When I got to Salisbury one of the things I did was get a subscription to the paper and had it sent home to my mother," Necciai says. "I told her that if she didn't see my name in the obits I was doing OK. My name wasn't in the obits but seeing the write ups of some of the games I pitched she must have wondered how I was staying alive.

"I got to the point to where I realized that playing baseball could be a good way to make a living. My mother could never understand someone getting paid to play baseball. There was a little Italian lady who lived across the alley from us and she told my mother, 'Ronnie is a reala nicea boy. He getta his name in the paper and noa killa anybody.'"

Necciai began to find his pitching groove as he continued to receive valuable lessons from Detore.

"We were at Lexington warming up and George said, 'Son, come over here.' So I walk over to where George was standing on the first base side. He pointed over to the Lexington team warming up along the third base side and he said, 'Son, pick out one of those players.' I wasn't sure what he wanted me to do that for but I pointed to an older fellow who happened to be player-manager Hal Harrigan. George says, 'Fine. Every time he comes up to the plate I want you to knock him down on his butt.'

"With my control I was pretty good at knocking guys down without even trying but I asked George why he wanted me to knock him down every time. George said, 'Because I want you to show those guys you are in control.' I said, 'But Skip, that guy is the manager.' George says, 'I don't care, knock him down.' So every time Harrigan came up I would knock him down. And that went on every game I pitched. George would have me pick out a particular player and I would knock him down. I look at baseball now and you can't hit anybody. You can't throw on the inside of the plate. Back then, it was all part of the game. The hitters accepted it just as long as you didn't throw behind them. Then they knew you were trying to hurt them."

A young Necciai would sometimes get a little too cocky for his own good when things were going well.

"Pud Miller was the player-manager at Hickory and he ended up winning the league batting title with something like a .425 average. I got him out a couple times and I was going to make certain he remembered who I was. I was going to throw one by him. Detore was on the bench and he nodded his head for me to throw a change or to get the ball out of the zone to where he couldn't hit it. I said, 'Nah. I'm going to let him really see what one looks like as it's going by his nose.' I don't know if he hit it through the fence or over the fence but it was gone. First home run anybody ever hit off me. I didn't know what happened."

Detore, in his calm manner, said: "Well, son?"

"Skip, I thought I could get it by him," Necciai said.

"Son, they pay me to think and you to pitch," Detore said as he turned and slowly walked away.

Necciai's second start, at home against Mooresville, was another loss - 11-8. Necciai allowed only six hits over seven innings while striking out 11 but walking an astounding 12 batters. Necciai may have been tempted to go back to playing in the field as he went 3-for-4 against Statesville in a game he pitched seven and two thirds innings of relief giving up nine hits and five walks. Necciai relieved in one more game before getting another start against Concord. Necciai took the 2-1 loss but went the full nine innings striking out seven and walking only two and scattering eight hits.

Necciai continued to pitch inconsistently and control was a major problem, as his won-loss record sank to 0-7. Once again he was relegated to the bullpen to work out his problems and hopefully regain his confidence. It must have worked. A brilliant relief appearance against Landis was followed by a seven-inning complete game three-hitter against Lexington on June 23 which was his first win of the season. He was also 3-for-4 at the plate. After another relief appearance, Necciai got his second win with a three-hit complete game against Concord striking out nine and walking only two.

Branch Rickey, Jr. was farm director for the Pirates and made a stop in Salisbury on July 21 to see another prospect but happened to catch Necciai in action. Despite losing to Elkin, 7-5, Necciai walked only four and struck out 13 in going the distance. After the game, Rickey spoke with Necciai in the clubhouse.

"I was 0-for-something as far as wins. I was really horse crap," Necciai admits. "Rickey, Jr. saw me pitch and I had a pretty good game. Rickey came in the clubhouse and dressed me down real good. He said I should be ashamed of myself to be in a league like this and to have a sorry record like I did. He told me to get my act together and then the Pirates would send me somewhere to where I could make some money. After Rickey left, George said, 'Son, you had that coming.' I admitted that I did have it coming."

Coincidence or not, Necciai began to turn his season around after that speech from Rickey. He won four in a row and was selected to pitch in the North Carolina State all-star game. But, he never stepped on the field with the all-stars. After hurling 106 innings over a 20 game span allowing 91 hits and striking out 111 batters, Necciai was leaving Salisbury. The Pirates, despite Necciai's high issue of walks with 87 and a 4-9 won-loss record, were sending the youngster to Class AA New Orleans of the Southern Association.

It was Rickey Jr.'s decision to send Necciai to New Orleans. A decision that Rickey Sr. questioned. "I watched this kid in several games," Rickey Jr. was quoted. "I knew the kid had the stuff. Won-loss records don't mean much. It's the ability in the box that counts. I returned to Forbes Field and told my dad that this kid had something. My dad was surprised when I told him I was going to move the kid to New Orleans but I argued anybody could tell by simply looking at him that he was a comer."

Necciai sat on the bench for the first ten days with his new club and in his first start hurled a five-hitter against Mobile, but lost 2-0. Necciai would struggle in the eight games he pitched for the Pelicans over 33 innings, allowing 44 hits and walking 42 while fanning just 11. Necciai's record was 1-5 and his ERA an inflated

8.45. Then, his season ended prematurely when he stumbled over first base and pulled a leg muscle with two weeks remaining.

"I was a little disappointed at New Orleans," Necciai says. "Rip

Ron Necciai with New Orleans (Courtesy Ron Necciai).

Sewell, the manager, didn't do anything with the guys as far as instruction. As you advance higher they assume you need less work and less coaching. They expect you to know things. Rip's theory was to knock them down and give them the Uncle Charley (curve). I really didn't learn anything and struggled during the brief time I was with the club.

"It was so different playing for Sewell and playing for Detore. George, who called me son, and I really looked upon him as a father, would go out at six in the morning if you asked him to help you work on a certain pitch or practice your pickoff throw to first base."

Necciai also credits roving minor league pitching coach Bill Burwell with helping him develop as a pitcher. "Whenever he came around our club, he spent as much time as he could with me. I really got good instruction from Burwell," Necciai says.

Under Sewell, who made the epheus pitch (the ball was thrown almost in slow motion, reaching a high apex halfway between the plate and the mound before dropping over the plate) famous during a 12-year career in Pittsburgh, the Pirates had several young pitchers of whom they had great expectations.

"The Pirates had a couple of other kids who were prospects and they wanted Sewell to work with us," Necciai recalls. "Ronnie Kline was there, Jim Koski, Jim Waugh. Three of us wound up with bad shoulders. When it came to game time, it was the same story for me. I struck out a few but I walked a lot."

Despite his less than impressive statistics at New Orleans, the Pirates were very high on Necciai. As a matter of fact, there were rumors of Necciai making the Pirates' big league roster in 1952. No less than Branch Rickey, the Pirates GM, said of Necciai: "There have been only two young pitchers I was certain were destined for greatness simply because they had the meanest fastball a batter can face. One of those boys was Dizzy Dean. The other is Ron Necciai and Necciai is harder to hit."

While the minor leagues were closing down for the 1951 season, the innovative Rickey brainstormed the idea of a fall baseball school for several of the Pirates young hopefuls. The theory behind the school was to speed up development of young players during what would be a 30-day camp in Deland. Necciai was one of those players who spent October in Florida. In the 30 days he was there, the Pirate scouts gave him a high evaluation. The camp would be a prelude to what would turn out to be an extraordinary 1952 season for Necciai.

Chapter 4

A Pitching Prospect

Acold February wind was whipping through the Monongahela Valley. Ron Necciai gave his mother a long embrace, told her he would write home every chance he got and then grabbed his small leather suitcase and walked out the door to where brother Til had the car running to take Ron into town and to the bus depot. The two brothers used to think nothing of walking the short distance from their home to downtown Monongahela. But today was different. As they both shivered from the cold, Til kidded Ron about being careful not to get sunburn in California.

Til parked in front of the depot, shook Ron's hand and watched as his little brother disappeared inside to purchase his one-way ticket for the 30-mile trip to Pittsburgh. It would be the first stage of a journey that would end in San Bernardino, California where the Pittsburgh Pirates conducted spring training for the big league club. The bus bounced up Route 88 making quick stops in Finleyville and Bethel Park before arriving at Pennsy Station in downtown Pittsburgh. Ron was a couple hours early of his departure time on the Pennsylvania Railroad, which would take a first wave of young Pirates to Chicago where they would travel over the Chicago and Northwest Lines to Omaha. From there the trip would transport the Pirates to Ogden, Utah and then the final leg of the California trip over the Union Pacific to San Bernardino.

As Necciai entered the station's cavernous lobby, he spotted Kenny Barbao and Tony Bartirome, a kid from the Hill District of Pittsburgh. The first squad of Pirates, comprised of young players considered to be major league prospects, was to begin spring training on Monday, February the 18th at Perris Hill Park in San Bernardino. Leaving late on Friday, the trip would take over two days. A second squad of Pirates, consisting mainly of those on the major league roster, was scheduled to report to camp on March 3. It was the first time for many of the youngsters on a Pullman and they reacted as teen-agers do when away from home. Plenty of talking and cutting up and not a lot of sleep. Bobby Del Greco, another Hill District product, Paul Smith from nearby Wilkinsburg and Ronnie Kline of Callery were among the contingent on this trip.

Danny Murtaugh, manager of the New Orleans farm club, joined the others in Chicago but not before loosening the crowd in Chicago's Northwestern Station. Murtaugh, an Irishman built like a fire hydrant with a devilish sense of humor, spotted two ladies nearby walking small dogs. Murtaugh began barking like a bulldog sending the smaller pups into a panic. The startled women wanted to give Murtaugh a piece of their mind but he and the Pirates boarded their train giggling and acting like school kids on an outing. The loose and relaxed atmosphere continued on the train as the players spent most of the time laughing and ribbing one another. It was way after midnight that traveling secretary Bob Rice convinced the young men to climb into their berths and get some rest. After encountering a snowstorm outside of Ogden that almost forced a stop in their travel, the Pirates arrived in San Bernardino. The frivolous mood of the players had been tempered somewhat by the long trip, but their mood had undergone a change as they realized some decorum was necessary before entering the team headquarters at the California Hotel.

The Pirates were a struggling organization. It was the intent of the owners and Branch Rickey to rescue the Pirates from a slide into oblivion. In the attempt to stop the slide the Pirates dished out nearly $600,000 in bonus money signing prospective young players. The largest check went to Frankie Van Burkleo, a 17 year old left-handed pitcher right out of high school, for whom the Pirates outbid the Chicago White Sox giving the youngster from Los Angeles a reported $40,000. Jim Waugh, a right-hand pitcher, was given $35,000 in June of 1951 and was 10-8 at Class D Brunswick of the Georgia-Florida League.

Dick Hall, the towering 6-foot-6 pitcher-infielder-outfielder from Swathmore College, received $30,000 and Gair Allie, a shortstop out of Wake Forest, also pocketed $30,000. Don Beitler, an infielder from Seton Hall, received a $30,000 bonus, as did pitcher Bill Bell. Lee Walls, an infielder, collected $25,000 the year before and hit .342 with Modesto of the Class C California League.

Spring training was the first step in placing these young players together and evaluating the talent. There was plenty of work ahead. The first man to greet the early arrivals was Branch Rickey. The scheduled routine was for the players to have morning practice sessions with intra-squad games in the afternoon for the next two weeks and ending on March 3, the date that the Pirate regulars were due to report. Supervising the daily workouts was Rickey himself.

As Rickey watched the prospects after only four hours on the field, he was inspired by their enthusiasm and athletic prowess. After the fifth day of camp, Rickey wired manager Bill Meyer back in Pittsburgh that he, Meyer, might want to come out a week early to catch these kids in action. Meyer was to report just ahead of the major league contingent but on Rickey's urging, Meyer changed his plans and headed for California.

It was common procedure for Rickey to gather his ballplayers and, like Boy Scouts around a campfire, lecture on various subjects. And Rickey always invited the reporters covering the Pirates to attend these sessions. It was rise at 7 a.m., eat breakfast and hear from Mr. Rickey. On the first day the subject was catching colds. Rickey's theory, and he directed it especially for those boys from back east, was that the eastern kids if they perspire and then stand in the shade are more likely to catch a cold. Whether there was any validity to this theory and why Rickey singled out the eastern kids is anyone's guess. But that was Rickey. Other subjects Rickey would lecture ranged from why they should keep their distance from women while in spring training to what to eat to keep their bodies strong and healthy.

Rickey also gave the boys a pep talk on patriotism.

"I realize that about half of you youngsters are holding 1-A cards and I would like to think that all of you who hold them are proud of them," Rickey was quoted in the *Pittsburgh Sun-Telegraph*. "There are few things in life that are more honorable than to fight for your country."

Over the next couple of years many of these young men would indeed be suiting up for their country rather than for their team as the United States was becoming involved in the Korean conflict. "Rickey didn't always talk about baseball," Necciai remembers.

Branch Rickey is all smiles with Necciai, left, and Tony Bartirome (Courtesy Ron Necciai).

"He would focus on life and how to conduct yourself. I thought he was the greatest speaker I ever heard. He could sell refrigerators to Eskimos. He'd give you one of his pep talks and you were ready to tear the walls down. He prodded me to do better. Mr. Rickey gave me every opportunity and encouraged me."

After Rickey would wax philosophical each morning, the players - a total of 27, 13 of which were pitchers - made their way to the diamond complex for the 10 a.m. calisthenics drill. From there it was fielding drills followed by lunch and then batting practice. Necciai was right there in his Pirate flannels with the number 54 on his back doing his best to impress the Pirate instructors and Mr. Rickey.

Rickey sincerely liked this group of prospects. Rickey could not help but rave about the likes of 18-year-old catcher Bob Flynn, who had never played in a professional game. Rickey was high on Van Burkleo and Bell, who Rickey was predicting could be in Pittsburgh that very year. Rickey was also touting Hall and Jackie Brown, who was scouted by Pie Traynor and who coach George Sisler said had the best curveball in camp. Walls, at 19, was being compared as a third baseman to Hall of Famer Traynor. When Meyer made his arrival he was somewhat more cautious than Rickey in his appraisals of the young Pirates but he too saw talent with promising potential. One of those talented players who caught Meyer's eye was Necciai, who did not receive a penny to sign.

As spring training started to wind down, the Pirates began assigning many of their rookies to the Triple A club in Hollywood and to Double A New Orleans. So far, Necciai wasn't one of those sent out. Rickey and his staff were impressed with Necciai and the possibility was real that he might make the trip to Pittsburgh when camp finally broke.

The Pirates were set to take on the defending National League champion New York Giants in an exhibition at Perris Hill Park and Meyer told Necciai to be ready because he would follow starter Howie Pollet to the mound.

With a lineup featuring Alvin Dark, Bobby Thomson, Monte Irvin and Willie Mays, the Giants were, arguably, the most feared hitting team in the National League. Pollet allowed no runs on two hits over the first four innings and was lifted to start the fifth with the score 0-0. Necciai, who was not listed on the Pirates 40-man roster, was summoned from the bullpen and for five innings held the Giants scoreless on two hits. The young pitcher walked only one batter and struck out two. For 10 innings Pollet and Necciai allowed no runs as Meyer and Rickey salivated over the prospects of this continuing once the regular season started. The Giants, however, appeared to be coming out on top scoring two runs off Paul LaPalme in the top of the 11th inning but Pittsburgh retaliated in the bottom of the 11th with three runs for the win.

On the final day of spring training before breaking for their barnstorming trip back east, the Pirates faced the St. Louis Browns at Perris Hill Park with Necciai given the starting assignment. But three St. Louis hits and three Necciai walks produced four first inning runs for the Browns. Necciai settled down shutting out St. Louis over the next three innings as he issued just one more walk and allowed no hits. This convinced Rickey and Meyer that Necciai would start the season on the major league roster.

"We were getting ready to break camp and Billy (Meyer) told me that I was staying with the big league club and would head east with the Pirates," Necciai says. "We left San Bernardino by train and we were traveling with the St. Louis Browns. We would barnstorm with the Browns along the way. Half the train was the Pirates and the other half of the train had the Browns with Paige, Bearden, Marty Marion and those guys."

But the pressure of maintaining a high performance level to remain with the Pirates began taking a toll. Necciai, admittedly, worried about everything.

"I did worry, I worried all the time," Necciai confesses. "I was so nervous that I would burn cigarettes faster than Chesterfield could make them. I had ulcers and the ulcers got worse as we made our way back east."

After playing a game against the Browns in Corpus Christi, Texas, the Pirates make their way to New Orleans. Meanwhile, the Browns diverted north and the Pirates began the second leg of

Necciai wears the Pirate uniform during spring training (Courtesy Ron Necciai).

their journey cross country playing the Chicago Cubs. Before stopping in New Orleans Necciai had pitched 15 innings, gave up seven runs on 14 hits, walked seven and struck out six. Before going out to pitch against the Chicago Cubs in New Orleans at Pelican Field Necciai slipped off to the restroom and was spitting up blood. He came out to pitch the ninth inning, faced eight Cub batters and was ripped for four runs on four hits, he walked one and had two wild pitches.

"Actually, I had been spitting blood all spring," Necciai says. "It was my ulcers which was a result of being nervous. I tried to keep it quiet but I was losing weight. I couldn't eat. Meyer noticed and so did Rickey. I guess that one bad inning at New Orleans was the last straw."

Necciai was sick. Too sick to play baseball. Pirates' team physician Dr. Norman C. Ochsenhirt recommended to the Pittsburgh front office, and to Necciai, that the pitcher enter Presbyterian Hospital in Pittsburgh. Necciai spent the next two weeks resting, putting on the weight he had lost, regaining his strength and trying to cope with that obsession called worry. When it was determined that Necciai was fit enough to begin pitching the Pirates assigned him to New Orleans, but Necciai never made it to Louisiana. The Pirates informed Necciai he would have to work himself back into shape and asked him where he would like to spend the next three or four weeks rehabilitating.

Necciai gave it some thought as to where he might be the most comfortable and he then asked one question: "Where was George Detore?" Wherever Detore was managing, that's where Necciai wanted to be. The idea was to rehabilitate back into playing condition and Necciai could think of no one better to play for than the man he had the utmost confidence in. Necciai's rehab was part physical and part mental. If he felt better with Detore, then that was okay with the Pirates.

When told that Detore was managing a Class D team in a small town in Virginia, Necciai didn't blink an eye. That was where he wanted to be.

"I was talking with Branch Rickey, Jr. and he told me the idea was for me to work myself back into shape," Necciai says. "I asked Mr. Rickey where Detore was managing and he said in Bristol,

Virginia. I didn't know where Bristol was. Never heard of it and I didn't know whether it was A or B or Z ball. I wanted to be where George was and I told Mr. Rickey that. He thought about it for a while and finally said, 'OK, then Bristol it is.' "

Chapter 5

Bound for Bristol

I n 1952 Bristol Tennessee-Virginia was the center of commerce in the foothills of the Appalachian Mountains. City merchants depended heavily upon the trade from the many residents who lived in the rugged coal fields of Southwest Virginia, some traveling over sixty miles on crooked two lane roads to shop for necessities. Bristol was also a strategic hub for goods traveling by railway from the north by way of Richmond and Roanoke to the southern stops in Knoxville, Chattanooga and Atlanta and Lee Highway was the main thoroughfare connecting North and South for travelers going by automobile.

Bristol had a population of approximately 25,000 and was surrounded by a very vibrant farming economy. Burley tobacco was the primary cash crop and the landscape was dotted with dairy farms and beef cattle grazing on the rolling hillsides.

Bristol, founded in 1856 and taking its name from Bristol England, was like any other small town across America except for the fact that Bristol was actually two towns, not one, with two city governing bodies with each side of town having its own police force and fire department. State Street ran directly down the middle of the main business district with one side of town sitting in Virginia and the other side of town in Tennessee. This anomaly was the reason why the local baseball team was called the Twins as Bristol was known as the Twin City. A semipro baseball team also borrowed its name - the Stateliners - from the fact Bristol was dissected by the state line of Virginia and Tennessee.

A photograph dating from the 1930s shows a Fourth of July parade and leading the parade were the governors of Virginia and Tennessee both waving from cars motoring down State Street. The cars progressed from one end of town to the other side-by-side separated by only the white line in the center of the street, as the governors never left their respective states of Virginia and Tennessee. Spanning the street near Union Station - the railroad depot - was a 60-foot sign touting Bristol as "A Good Place To Live." After dark, lights on the sign formed arrows pointing downward to the street below. Below one arrow was VA and below the other TENN, just in case a visitor was wondering which side of the state line he or she might be on.

Before the era of malls, television and computers, people actually strolled the sidewalks window shopping at H.P. King's - the largest retailer between Roanoke and Knoxville - stocking items ranging from clothes to kitchen appliances to toys in a mammoth three-story building. A man could get a haircut for a dollar at Sanitary Barbershop, billed as Bristol's Largest and Most Modern Barbershop. Bunting's Drug Store was always crowded at lunch with downtown workers on break ordering up the store's delectable hot dog smothered in chili and onions with a cherry Coke to wash it down. Saturday afternoon was when the kids flooded the theatres to watch a movie at the Paramount, Cameo,

Lee, Shelby or Columbia. Or you might even catch such silver screen heroes as Gene Autry or Tex Ritter performing in person on stage. Lash LaRue was one of those western actors who came to town but ended up in a brawl at one of the local bars when confronted by an inebriated patron who wanted to take on the lasso-throwing cowboy. It never made the paper but some rumors have it that LaRue was challenged by a member of the Bristol Twins who wanted to see if the cowboy was as tough as he was on the big screen slugging it out with the villains.

Bristol was also a town steeped in musical heritage. In 1927, in what has become known at The Bristol Sessions, hillbilly bands came together, including legends such as A.P. Carter and Jimmie Rodgers, and recorded for Victor records and from that was the start of country music. Bristol today is known as The Birthplace of Country Music. In 1919, Ernest Ford was born in Bristol, Tennessee on Anderson Street. Little Ernie had a fascination with music and would sing in the choir at Anderson Street Methodist Church. Ernest, with a silky baritone voice, would become known simply as Tennessee Ernie selling millions of records and becoming a television star of the 1950s and 60s.

It was during the decades of the 1940s and 1950s that baseball swept across America as major league franchises developed farm systems utilizing small towns, such as Bristol, to drill young ballplayers in the basics of the game. Bristol entered professional baseball in 1911 and through the years had been affiliated as a Class D farm club of the New York Yankees, New York Giants and the Pittsburgh Pirates. Among the players who wore the Twins' uniform were Bobby Thomson, who hit the home run to win the pennant for the Giants in 1951, and Bobby Cain, who pitched for the Chicago White Sox against the St. Louis Browns the day owner Bill Veeck had midget Eddie Gaedel pop out of a huge birthday cake and take his turn at bat.

About two miles from Bristol's main business district stood Shaw Stadium, home of the Bristol Twins. Shaw Stadium was a rustic wooden structure constructed in 1943 and from early May to late August the ballpark hosted 60 Appalachian League games. On the 1952 Bristol Twins program Shaw Stadium was billed as: *Where the Stars of Tomorrow Play Tonight.*

The local team was deemed worthy of such coverage that the daily newspaper - *The Bristol Herald Courier* - delegated sports editor Gene Thompson to Florida to cover the Pirates at their minor league camp in Deland. It was through Thompson's reports that fans back in Bristol could read in-depth accounts about the team, which eventually would be spending the summer in Bristol and whose players were treated like family. It was also through Thompson's writings that the fans in Bristol first heard of Ron Necciai. Necciai arrived late in Deland after his hospital stay in Pittsburgh and was able to only get in a couple of weeks of training. Thompson kept hearing about this kid who some said threw as fast, if not faster, than Feller. Thompson, as were many, was skeptical at such reports so he asked Bill Burwell, former big league pitcher and former minor league manager who was serving as a minor league coach for the Pirates in spring training, about the hard-throwing Necciai.

"Necciai has all the assets to become a great major league pitcher. He has terrific speed and a great curveball," Thompson quoted Burwell. "He's young and needs poise and the polish that comes with experience but he definitely is one of the better pitching prospects in baseball today."

Thompson still wasn't convinced and decided to seek a second opinion, asking Bristol manager George Detore about this young pitcher who sounded like a character from a Zane Grey novel.

"Necciai has everything but experience to become a major league winner," Detore analyzed. "He has a live fastball and one of the best fast-breaking curves I have ever seen. I saw some of the top right-handers, including Monte Pearson, and I rate Necciai's fast curve as good, if not better, than that of Pearson's. He needs to correct a fault with his overhand fastball, he needs to gain better control of his curve and we are going to help him develop his sidearm pitch. In fact, I think that his sidearm stuff may be his greatest asset in time. We feel that he definitely will become one of the top pitchers on the Pittsburgh club."

These two men, who had solid reputations judging baseball talent, were giving some glowing testimonials for a teen-ager who, only a year before, was ready to give up the game. It was rare the club would go out on the limb and predict success for someone so unproven but the feeling around the Pirates' camp was that Necciai was a rare gem.

"I know I kept thinking, 'Are they talking about me?' " Necciai says. "I hadn't done anything in baseball and they were already putting me in the major leagues, at least to hear them talk. But, I liked hearing it."

The plan for Necciai was to pitch Bristol's opening game of the season against the Kingsport Cherokees and then pitch every fourth day in a set rotation. After a month, the Pirates would evaluate Necciai's progress and then decide if a promotion higher up the minor league chain or even perhaps to the big league club in Pittsburgh was warranted.

As the team broke spring training camp at Deland to travel north by bus on their two-day journey to Bristol with an overnight stay in Atlanta, the finishing touches were being applied to Shaw Stadium in preparation of the season's opener on May 2. The grass was getting a fresh cut, the concession stands were being stocked and the outfield signs were getting a new coat of paint.

Detore and the Bristol Twins arrived in late afternoon with the bus belching diesel fumes as it pulled onto the cinder covered parking lot just beyond the third base side of Shaw Stadium. The players followed Detore off the bus and into the stadium through the left field gate. The clubhouse was located down the third base line on a small rise beyond the bleachers. It was a crude structure but not unlike what Necciai had seen at some of his previous stops in Salisbury and Shelby. It was definitely Class D standards. Once inside the clubhouse there was a nail to hang the uniform, a stool on which to sit, a table with a couple of chairs around it in the center of the room and one large shower stall. Near the door and off to one side was a small office for the manager.

After unloading equipment the players and Detore boarded the bus again bound across town to Hotel Bristol located opposite Union Station. Hotel Bristol would be the temporary home for the players until they could find permanent quarters for the summer. Finding accommodations for the summer wasn't too difficult as several families year after year would open their homes to board players for a fee cheaper than staying in a hotel. It would be at Hotel Bristol the next day that the Lions Club officially rolled out the welcome mat for the young players before the Twins held their first workout at Shaw Stadium.

Most minor league towns treated the young players like stars and Bristol was certainly no exception giving the team the royal treatment with an evening banquet. The next day would be all business for the players. The Twins would waste little time in diving into a game situation as Saturday the Twins were scheduled to play an exhibition against a semi-pro team in Saltville Virginia. And, on Sunday afternoon at Shaw, Necciai was scheduled to pitch against Batavia, New York of the Class D Pony League, another Pittsburgh affiliate. But rain postponed the trip to Saltville and the rain continued the next day canceling the exhibition against Batavia.

All the Twins could do was sit and wait for the clouds to move out. The squad that left Deland was made up of, along with Necciai, pitchers Ronnie May, Bill Huefler, Kenneth Miller, Paul Hensley, Tiny Jenkins, Tom Smith, Angelo Orlando and Frank Ramsay. The catchers were Harry Dunlop and Don Becker. Comprising the infield delegation were Philip Filiatrault, Ed Burch, Don DeVeau, and Joe Novotniak. Outfielders consisted of Bob Lipstas, Bob Chrisley, Charlie Greenhill and Bill Gelsinger. Fifteen of those players were in their first year of professional baseball. Before the end of the season some would be cut and some would move up the minor league ladder and new players would join the team during the course of the summer.

Necciai would forge a strong relationship with his teammates, especially the 18-year-old Dunlop. Dunlop, a 6-foot-2, 187-pound catcher was considered by scouts one of the top defensive receivers in the Pirates' minor league system based on what scouts saw of him in spring training. The Pirates felt Dunlop would be the perfect match for Necciai whose control, at best, was erratic. Whoever caught Necciai would be scooping curves out of the dirt and chasing fastballs to the screen. Detore was counting on Dunlop to be a stabilizing factor, not only for Necciai, but for his entire pitching staff. A solid defensive catcher was a key in the development of pitchers.

The rain eventually subsided and the Twins bused to Saltville, a small town about 45 minutes north of Bristol once known as the Salt Capital of the Confederacy during the Civil War, to play the Alkalies. The Alkalies, a semi-pro team in the Burley Belt League, beat the Twins 11-10 in 12 innings in a game that lasted over three hours. Necciai sat on the bench next to Detore and observed as Ronnie May debuted allowing just two hits over five innings before being lifted. Bill Huefler went the final six and two thirds losing the game on a sacrifice fly. If the weather held, the Twins would play what would be their only exhibition game of the preseason at Shaw Stadium against the Elizabethton Tennessee Ramblers, also of the Burley Belt League. It would be Necciai's turn to take the mound for a pre-season warm-up.

The rain stopped but under the lights at Shaw Stadium the night turned cold and damp. Necciai went to the mound and gave a performance matching the hype which trailed him from Florida. Necciai struck out eight, walked three and allowed just one hit over three innings before developing a blister on the middle finger of his right hand. Detore didn't want Necciai pitching with a blister in a game that meant nothing, so the Bristol manager called in Frank Ramsay to relieve. Ramsay, who finished the 1951 season with Norton Virginia of the Mountain States League, struck out the first five batters he faced and finished with 11 strikeouts for the night as Bristol won 12-4.

As Detore leaned back in the dugout watching his young pitchers, he felt he had a staff with unlimited potential. However, Detore knew he had to be careful to temper his excitement to the press or to the pitchers themselves. Kids with swelled heads and

The Cherokees, a farm club of the New York Giants, jumped on May for three first inning runs. Detore left the struggling young left-hander on the mound to work out his own problems. Detore had learned patience over the years. The successful managers in the lower minor leagues all learn patience. A struggling pitcher who couldn't find the plate or a hitting prospect going through a 0-for-20 streak had to keep playing. Nothing kills the confidence of a young player more than to be pulled and relegated to the bench.

Often a player with the tools had to fall down before he could walk. Detore was encouraged by what he observed of May who pitched the first five innings giving up six hits and striking out five. Detore told a reporter that May showed lots of poise. A good start for the young pitcher from Tacoma, Washington. In the Twins 9-3 loss to the Cherokees Bristol managed but four hits and three of those were by third baseman and Pittsburgh area native Joe Novotniak.

It had been a long day with the game ending close to 11 o'clock and it was nearly midnight before the team bus pulled onto the parking lot at Shaw Stadium. The players filed into the clubhouse, changed out of their gray flannel uniforms and then it was back on the bus for the short drive over to Hotel Bristol. It was almost two in the morning before Necciai put his head on the pillow and it was even later than that before he fell asleep with Detore's voice still reverberating: "You have to get ahead in the count kid. Don't be afraid to throw a curve on a 2-0 count. Keep the ball on the corner of the plate......"

Despite a lack of sleep, Necciai still awoke early the next morning. He, Dunlop and outfielder Bob Chrisley learned of a widow who was taking in ballplayers for the summer. They drove the few blocks from Hotel Bristol over to 500 Spruce Street, the home of Mabel Hagy, whose husband King, a professor of German at nearby King College, had passed away just a few months before. Boarding ballplayers in her home was an opportunity to take in a few dollars and she had a soft spot in her heart for these kids out on their own for the first time. She had three upstairs rooms at $5 a week and the players would have use of the kitchen downstairs. The three teammates agreed it would be more than suitable for their purposes for the summer and the price was one that their meager earnings as ballplayers could afford. They informed Mrs. Hagy that they would move in the next morning.

The trio left the house to explore downtown Bristol and ended up on Moore Street at Trayer's Restaurant owned and operated by a robust man in his early 40s by the name of Jack Trayer. Trayer was born in Daves, West Virginia and moved to Bristol in 1927 to open his restaurant. Trayer's restaurant would be a regular hangout for the ballplayers, as Trayer would often tear up their tickets after seeing them rummaging through their pockets for enough change to pay their bill.

The aromatic smell of hickory smoked barbecue filled the restaurant as the trio sat in a corner booth. Necciai, however, had this burning in his stomach. It was game day. He was a little apprehensive thinking about his start on the mound in just a few hours. As usual, when Necciai began to worry, the ulcers would start burning deep down. Necciai ordered a glass of milk and a cheese sandwich but left most of it on his plate. He went back to the hotel, tried to relax on the bed filling the ashtray with cigarette butts.

The ballplayers were to report to the park at three in the afternoon except for the starting pitcher, and he didn't have to show until four. But Necciai decided to get to the park early. It was better than the hotel room where it would be just he and his jittery nerves.

As he entered the left field gate at Shaw, Necciai looked around the park with its covered grandstand and a small pressbox perched on the roof behind home plate. Down the left field line, above the fence, was a wooden, hand-operated scoreboard. Necciai walked to the clubhouse and, upon entering, Detore motioned for him to come into his small office. Detore had been reading the morning paper but put it down on the desk to chat with Necciai and check and see how the blister on his finger was healing.

Detore sensed the youngster was nervous and he wanted to assure Necciai that he had nothing to prove. Just go out and pitch and try to attack each batter just liked they discussed on the bench. If the blister became a problem, make sure he let Dunlop know immediately. But, for now, the blister from the exhibition game wasn't a big concern.

The Twins' opener at Shaw Stadium was page-one news in the *Herald Courier*. Necciai scanned the paper in front of his locker before putting on his white flannel uniform with Twins emblazoned across the chest, a dark blue number 19 on the back and a cap with a large block B on the front. Game time was set for 7:45 p.m. and fans began trickling into the park when the gates opened at 6. The other Twins had been on the field limbering up as Necciai sat in the dugout. Dunlop trotted off the field, sat next to Necciai and asked how he was feeling. Necciai said fine but Dunlop could see Necciai was disguising his anxieties. Dunlop assured Necciai everything would be just dandy and to have fun. The two young batterymates strolled to the bullpen down the left field line to begin

Necciai, left, and Bristol catcher Harry Dunlop (United Press International Photo/Temple University Libraries, Urban Archives).

warming up. Necciai had a good pop to his fastball Dunlop thought, even though Necciai wasn't cutting loose all the way.

The game was only a few minutes from the opening ceremonies and the fans were buzzing in the stands at 7:40 as Necciai and his teammates took the field. On the mound to share

74

in tossing out the first pitch were Pittsburgh assistant farm director Bill Turner, Bristol Tennessee mayor Fred Vance and Bristol Virginia mayor Robert Kell. Dunlop received the pitch from each of the three and it was time to play ball.

Necciai tossed his warmup pitches to Dunlop as the infield of first baseman Philip Filiatrault, second baseman Ed Burch, shortstop Don DeVeau and third baseman Joe Novotniak were just as anxious and nervous as Necciai. As Kingsport leadoff batter Morton Epstein stepped to the plate, Necciai rubbed the baseball with his long fingers and faced the outfield. He glanced at his fielders - Chrisley in left, Gelsinger in center and Greenhill in right - before turning around to receive the sign from Dunlop behind the plate.

Relying only on his fastball, Necciai struck out Epstein on three pitches. For Epstein, it would prove to be a miserable night as he struck out four times. Standing in the dugout Detore nodded in approval and shouted a few encouraging words to Necciai. Almost two hours later over 2,400 fans left Shaw Stadium talking about that young kid with the unusual name. In a 4-0 Bristol victory, Necciai fanned 20 Cherokees, striking out eight straight during one stretch, and allowing only two hits. Necciai was just one strikeout shy of establishing an Appalachian League record set in 1945 by Elizabethton's Bob Kuhlman who fanned 21 Johnson City Cardinals. Even Detore was impressed with Necciai's performance despite the four bases on balls Necciai allowed.

In a column for his newspaper the next day, Gene Thompson wrote: "Necciai's new 20-game strikeout record for a Bristol pitcher should stand for a long time - unless he breaks it himself before he leaves."

In the home dugout Ronnie Odum, who won the batboy contest in the *Bristol Herald Courier* after over 7,000 ballots were cast, was enjoying every minute of this evening. In the visitor's dugout batboy Ken Draper, who was runner-up in the contest, watched silently as the Cherokee hitters made the slow frustrating walk back to the dugout from home plate.

There wasn't much said in the Cherokee dugout. An occasional curse, the slamming of a bat and just a sense of frustration. The Cherokees had never faced anyone quite like Necciai. The fans were enjoying this exhibition of pitching. They had read about Necciai and his overpowering fastball and baffling curve and it was very apparent to everyone in Shaw Stadium that this skinny kid could pitch. And the fans knew that if he repeated this type of performance every time he took the mound that he wouldn't be staying around Shaw Stadium very long.

"The plans were for Ronnie to stay a few weeks in Bristol and then move on up," Detore said in 1982 during a visit to Bristol. "It was evident after that first outing he would be leaving in a short time, providing he stayed healthy. Everybody knew that, even the fans."

Necciai was back on the Shaw Stadium mound five days later to start against the visiting Pulaski (Virginia) Phillies. Pulaski jumped out to a 2-0 first inning lead utilizing a hit, a walk and an error. Bristol then scored three in the bottom half and Necciai held the Phillies without a run for the next six innings. The Twins won 7-4 as Necciai struck out 19 hitters, striking out the side in the second, third and seventh innings. It was during the ninth inning that Necciai's unpredictable control went haywire as he walked three men to load the bases after two were out. However, he snuffed out the threat by fanning Roger Craver.

Detore was pleased with Necciai's overpowering fastball and congratulated the youngster but was quick to point out that the six bases-on-balls were way too many. Detore sat Necciai down and had a father and son chat explaining that six free passes was a result of just not concentrating, especially in the ninth inning walking three after two were out.

In a move that would never happen today with top prospects, Detore brought Necciai in to relieve starter Dick Orlando just three days later pitching four innings at Shaw against Johnson City. Necciai saved a 5-4 win for the Twins striking out 11, walking one and allowing no hits.

Bob Chrisley, whose brother Neil spent time in the major leagues, had played with Necciai in Salisbury in 1951 and formed a strong bond and a healthy respect for Necciai both as a friend and as a pitcher.

"Ron was a class act and he would pitch every day if you let him. Back in those days you started and relieved because you had so few pitchers on the staff," says Chrisley who roomed with Necciai and Dunlop and who used his signing bonus to buy a 1951 Chevrolet convertible, which the trio piled into for the trip to the ballpark every afternoon. "I named my son Ronald after Necciai. He had all the tools to pitch in the major leagues. If he could just get his control harnessed. The batter could tell what was coming and still couldn't hit Ron. When he went on the mound, he took over. He was a competitor."

Despite the ulcers, Necciai was feeling good physically. Most of the time the banthine pills settled his stomach along with milk and melba toast. And most days the ulcers weren't a problem. He was throwing the ball with tremendous velocity and Necciai was progressing just as the Pirates had envisioned. The organization had plans for the young right-hander and he appeared to be right on schedule.

Detore was thinking that Necciai was almost too good to be true. Detore felt like pinching himself to make sure he wasn't dreaming. But Detore and the fans hadn't seen anything yet. The best was yet to come.

Chapter 7

The Whiff Kids

When Necciai awoke about nine in the morning, he glanced at the calendar on the wall. It was Tuesday, May 13 and he had scribbled Welch on that date. The Welch Miners, located in the coal mining region of West Virginia about 30 miles west of Bluefield and a farm club of the Boston Braves, were in Bristol to play the first of a two game series that night at Shaw Stadium. Necciai was pencilled in for his third start of the season.

It was early in the day and already those persistent ulcers were burning. Necciai never complained openly. He didn't have too. He couldn't hide the pain when they hit and anyone who saw him knew immediately when the ulcers were flaring. He swallowed a banthine pill but that little tablet wasn't always the magic potion. Sometimes the ulcers didn't respond to the medication. He was even on a special diet which, among other things, excluded raw fruit, vegetables, fried foods, coffee, tea or carbonated drinks. It wasn't easy staying away from those foods, especially the fried foods, a staple of southern cooking. Being a ballplayer, Necciai

79

often ate on the go and sometimes it was a couple of hot dogs from the concession stand.

Necciai lit a Chesterfield, finished the smoke while listening to the radio, took a bath, shaved, dressed and went outside for some fresh air. It was a cool May morning and the smell of spring was very different than back home. The air here was clean and fresh, unlike the smoke-filled air he had become accustomed to while growing up around Gallatin. Necciai loved the spring. He couldn't help but think how beautiful this part of the country was. The grass was a lush green, the trees were budding and the tulips were the colors of a rainbow.

It was amazing, Necciai thought, how one year could make such a difference. He remembered his first season in pro ball and how disgusted he was with the game and actually gave it up to work in the mills. Now, he couldn't be happier. If it weren't for those aggravating ulcers life would be almost perfect. Necciai was actually enjoying the game more than ever. Standing on the sidewalk just outside the door of his boarding house, Necciai puffed on another Chesterfield as Dunlop came out the door going for a morning walk around the neighborhood.

Necciai joined Dunlop. Perhaps a stroll around the block might burn off some of that nervous energy. Necciai had forged a friendship with Dunlop and just talking with his battery mate seemed to be a calming influence. They talked about their futures wondering where baseball might take them both. Neither had reached their 20th birthday and there was still a great, big world to conquer.

Dunlop would never play in the major leagues but he would make a career of the game. Dunlop would spend 21 years as a major league coach with the Kansas City Royals, Chicago Cubs,

Cincinnati Reds, San Diego Padres and the Florida Marlins. In 2005 Dunlop actually managed a couple of games for the Marlins in the absence of manager Jack McKeon. In 1952, Dunlop, from Sacramento, California, was 18 and Necciai 19. Both were just kids with dreams.

"Sure, we were just kids having a good time playing baseball," Dunlop remembers. "We had never met until we both got to Bristol and then we roomed together and got to be very, very good friends. Ron had a fantastic arm. In those days we didn't have radar guns. I don't know for sure how hard he threw but from my experience I would say he threw in the upper 90s with a live fastball.

"Ron's fastball wasn't straight, it had life. His curve was almost like an old fashion drop. Almost like a split finger, it dropped that much. He was basically a two-pitch pitcher. He had the combination of that explosive fastball and then a curve that would drop right off the table. Ron had really long fingers and he could wrap those fingers around the ball and there was no strain on his elbow. Ron also could split his fingers, much like Bruce Sutter did a few years back. The fastball and curve would look the same for the first 60 feet."

Dunlop also points out that Necciai may have been the hardest guy on the Bristol staff to catch.

"He never got anybody out 1-2-3," Dunlop says. "There were a lot of 3-1 counts. He was hard to catch, but he was fun to catch at the same time. For as hard as he threw, and don't ask me to explain, but he threw a light ball. He threw hard but the ball was soft when it hit my mitt. It didn't feel like an eight-pound shot. I know one time he crossed me up. I called for a curve, he thought I called for a fastball. Ron threw the ball low all the time and with a curve I was anticipating the ball hitting the dirt. He threw the fastball. Well, I had the mitt going down and instinctively I reached out with my bare hand and caught his fastball. If he threw that hard I wouldn't have caught for two weeks."

Dunlop was the perfect match for Necciai. Detore recognized the duo's compatibility from day one.

"George was a great manager," Dunlop says. "He really knew baseball. George had me hitting cleanup in that Bristol lineup. I wasn't a power hitter and that's where you usually stick your power guy. I had never hit that many home runs. I told George I had never hit cleanup, not even in high school and was he sure he wanted me hitting fourth. George said, 'Harry, you're the one guy on this club who's going to make contact. That's why you're hitting cleanup.' George gave me, an 18-year-old kid, confidence. I have never forgotten many of the things that George told me. He's one big reason why I had such a long career in baseball.

"George taught me more about the position than anybody who ever coached me," Dunlop says. "He would get Ron and myself together and talk to us both at the same time. I think that's one reason that Ron and I had such a good rapport."

Necciai learned quickly that his success was going to depend on his having confidence in Dunlop behind the plate and in Dunlop having confidence in him on the mound.

"Harry was, and is, a real smart baseball man," Necciai says of Dunlop. "He was just 18 years old, but he was baseball smart. I remember George got us together one time and said, 'This is not a democracy. This is a dictatorship and I'm the dictator. We're going to do things my way.'

"But Harry had a helluva memory. Whatever the batter hit or chased the first time up, Harry remembered the second time